HILL COUNTRY CHRONICLES

by John Pape

HILL COUNTRY CHRONICLES

Sophisticated Tales of Life
in the
Texas Hill Country

by John Pape

Illustrated by
JoAnn Pape

First Edition 1992
Copyright 1992 by John Pape

All Rights Reserved. No part of this book may be reproduced in any form without written permission from the copyright owner or publisher, except for brief passages included in reviews appearing in a newspaper or magazine.

Contact Nel-Mar Publishing.
ISBN # 1-877740-18-7
Published and printed in the United States of America

Library of Congress Cataloging-in-Publication Data

Pape, John, 1956-
    Hill Country Chronicles : Sophisticated tales of life in the Texas Hill Country / by John Pape ; illustrated by JoAnn Pape. -- 1st ed.
    p. cm.
    ISBN 1-877740-18-7 (v. 1)
    1. Texas Hill Country (Tex.) -- Social life and customs -- Anecdotes.
I. Title.
F392.T47P37 1992
976.4--dc20   92-16978
                                                                CIP

Nel-Mar Publishing
HC-2, Box 267-C
Canyon Lake, Texas 78133
(512) 935-2420

DEDICATION

This book is dedicated to the three people who have given me everything good in life -

"Oma" Norma Thompson

"Opa" James Thompson

JoAnn Pape

My grandparents, James and Norma Thompson - Oma and Opa in the book - raised me. At a time in their lives when they should have had their time to themselves, they instead took in a "fat little blonde kid" of a grandson and gave him the love and guidance he needed to grow into a man.

My wife, JoAnn Pape, is more responsible for my successes in life than I. It was JoAnn who had the faith and confidence in my writing ability to convince me that other people would enjoy my stories of the Texas Hill Country.

There is no way I can ever repay these three people for what they have done for me, and mere words are a wholly - inadequate way to say "thank you". I can only be there for them as they have always been there for me, and this dedication is only a small token of my love and my respect.

ACKNOWLEDGMENTS

To Kit Brenner, "Newspaper Editor Extraordinaire" -

You had enough faith in my writing to be the first to run my column, and you stood by me no matter how outrageous I've gotten. You will always be a special part of my writing memories.

To Bodo Schwamkrug, Elroy Dietert, and all of the other characters who regularly appear in my "Chronicles" -

Thank you for sharing your lives with me and being good- natured enough to let me share some of those times with my readers.

To the readers of:

The Hill Country Recorder - Boerne, Texas
The Helotes Echo - Helotes, Texas
The Hays County Free Press - Buda, Texas
The Devine News - Devine, Texas

Thank you for reading, laughing at, reminiscing with, complaining about, screaming at, and lining your bird cages with my column over the last few years.

TABLE OF CONTENTS

INTRODUCTION
1   The Hill Country

SPRINGTIME IN THE HILL COUNTRY
5   Springtime: A Renewal
9   Oscar
13   Watermelon Time
15   Outhouses
17   About Cedar-Choppers
20   The King of Western Swing
24   Belly-up to the Worm Bar
27   Gold in Them Thar Hills?
30   Bodo Schwamkrug's in Love
34   Uncle Herbert's Still
37   Night of the Killing Waters

SUMMER IN THE HILL COUNTRY
41   Sky King & Me
44   Mr. Ebell's Cave
47   A Golf Bet with God
53   Save the Outhouse!
56   Tank Fishing
58   Unlucky Lindy
60   Porch Sittin' Talk
62   Riding in the Bed of a Pickup Truck
66   Die Scheutzenverein
68   Emma's New Outhouse
72   My Father - the Bullfighter
76   "God Bless You, For Spotty and Me"

AUTUMN IN THE HILL COUNTRY
- 80   The Infamous Chicken-Suit Caper
- 84   Roadside Dinosaurs
- 86   Bodo Rides Again
- 89   Katzenmusik
- 91   Vote for Bonehead
- 94   Bodo's Deer Hunt
- 98   Combat School-Bus Driving
- 101   To Schwartz, or Not to Schwartz . . .
- 104   Friday Night Fever
- 109   County Fair
- 111   Trick or Treat
- 116   Oma

WINTER IN THE HILL COUNTRY
- 120   Agapito's Pig
- 124   A Modern-Day Dinosaur
- 128   Mrs. Davis' Sunday School Lesson
- 131   Pannas - Breakfast of Champions
- 134   Mail-Order Alligator
- 138   Rambo Meets Bambi
- 142   Hometown Radio - A Blast From the Past
- 146   A Cedar-Chopper's Christmas
- 150   What's in a Name?
- 153   A Place in Time
- 157   Martha's Birthday
- 160   Big Oma

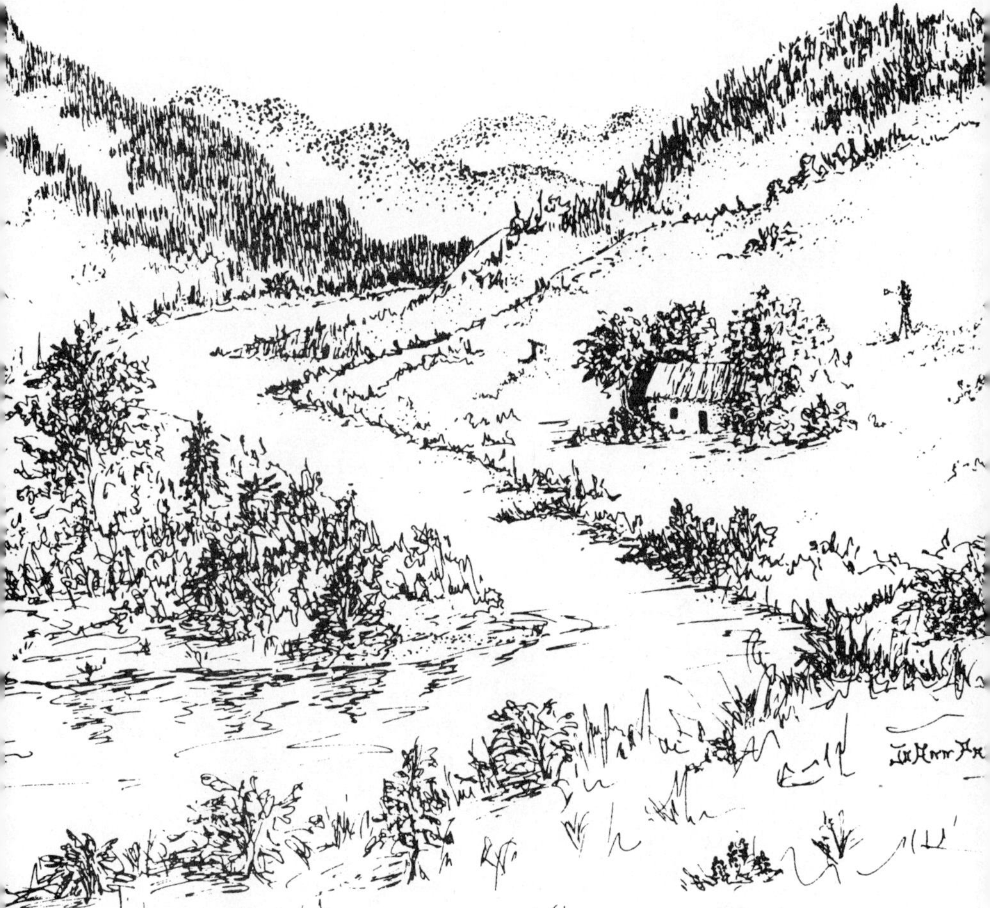

THE HILL COUNTRY

"They are timeless, these places - dreamlike, yet indestructible. They are intrusions of immortality into the random flow of daily life. They should not matter, but they do. And, once perceived, they glow, stubbornly, like hoarded treasures, in the attic of the mind."

"This Favored Place"

by Eloy Bode

The passage above was written about the Texas Hill Country, a place difficult to imagine but impossible to forget. This is what "Hill Country Chronicles" is all about. It is a celebration of the Hill Country - the people, places, heritage, and culture of a region that has given us Presidents and poets; bandits and balladeers; heroes and homefolks; champions and cedar choppers.

It is a look at ourselves with warmth, fondness, reminiscence, occasional reproach, and a liberal dose of humor as we recall our traditions and our people - some famous, most obscure. It is a telling of the tales of the English,

Germans, Mexicans, Indians, Italians, Irish, Czechs, Poles, and all of the other immigrants that, together, formed the fabric that binds us together as Texans. And it is a celebration of the land - harsh, yet giving; sparse, yet lush - that is as much a part of us as our soul.

I must admit to not having truly appreciated the Hill Country until I had left the area. I quickly realized that the Hill Country was neither the norm nor the inferior, but rather the kind of place people want to be a part of.

The Hill Country of my youth included as many people speaking German as English. A trip into the countryside was, to a youthful mind, an expedition into a vast, beautiful wilderness. A trip up Bear Creek Road meant a dusty drive with a pause alongside the clear waters of the creek for a picnic. The trip was capped with a visit to Emma Rieber and her "Indian Days House" for a bowl of Emma's home-made chili. Emma sold many a bowl of chili and, rumor had it, even had a hand in fighting off an Indian or two in her younger days.

The weekends would mean a trip to Sattler so my grandparents could socialize and bowl nine-pin at the two-lane bowling alley. One of my first great aspirations was to be a pin boy at the Sattler bowling alley but, with only two lanes, not many vacancies occurred.

English was pretty much a foreign language at these gatherings. As German punctuated the warm evening air, there was an opportunity for my family members from Hancock and Hidden Valley to visit with those who had left the hills for the "city life" of New Braunfels or Fredericksburg.

Today, old Hancock lies beneath the waters of Canyon Lake and exists only in the memories of those of us who are somehow tied to its past. Hidden Valley exists only as an opening between hilltop subdivisions, allowing the tourists a picture-postcard view of Canyon Dam. Emma and her home-made chili are gone. The Indians are gone as well - possibly because of the intervention of Emma and her chili - most probably as a result of the progress that has engulfed us all.

The Hill Country of my childhood no longer exists. Maybe it never did. Maybe my childhood memories, coupled with my adult reflections, have made this all nothing more than a candy-coated illusion. Maybe. But I refuse to surrender those memories to the harsh light of reason.

The popularity of the Hill Country must prove that more than one set of dreams have drifted lazily down the, Medina, Guadalupe or Frio on a summer's afternoon. I only hope that everyone who comes here looking for a better way of life develops his or her own personal relationship with the land. That relationship is the most special part of life in the Hill Country. It is a relationship that will last you a lifetime.

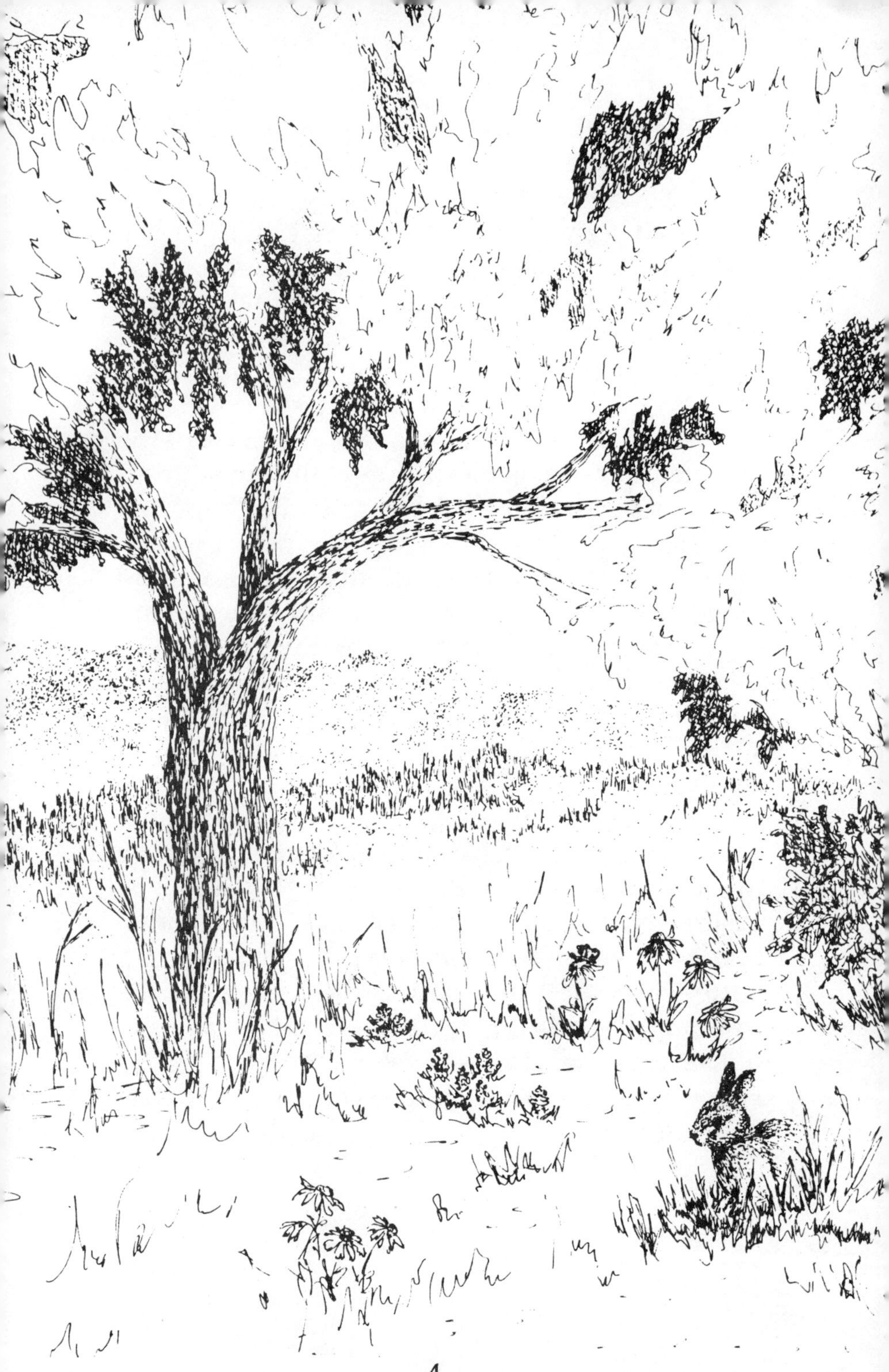

SPRINGTIME IN THE HILL COUNTRY

*****

SPRINGTIME : A RENEWAL

All of the seasons have a special feeling in the Hill Country. The warm days of summer invite you to lie by a cool stream beneath a spreading pecan tree; the first frost of Autumn brings a feeling of anticipation and change; the cold, brisk morning air of Winter tells of a world asleep, awaiting rebirth. But of all the seasons, my favorite has to be Spring.

Springtime in the Hill Country is a time of renewal. The browns of Winter give way to a green carpet of new growth across the hillsides. Within a few weeks, the native wildflowers will paint a mosaic of color across the landscape. The world is, once again, alive.

Springtime - the renewal of the land.

When I was growing up, springtime also meant dewberries, ripe for the picking. On many Spring mornings, we would get up at dawn and head for the banks of the Guadalupe River where the dewberries grew wild and plentiful. There, in the cool of the morning along the river bank, my family would fill buckets with fresh dewberries. More dewberries were eaten than gathered, but it was the occasion that was special, not how much we collected.

Living on a farm, Springtime also meant birth. Night-long vigils were often rewarded with the arrival of a new colt or calf. Chickens, turkeys, and ducks were, quite literally, hatching out all over. Even the dogs and cats produced offspring that became part of the annual renewal.

Springtime - the renewal of God's dominion.

It was during the Springtime that Mr. Robinson came by our place for his first visit of the season. I suppose that Mr. Robinson was the first black man I ever saw. Every year, he would come from Luling with his pickup truck loaded down with more fruits and vegetables than you could ever imagine. Of particular interest to my grandmother were his watermelons and cantaloupes.

Mr. Robinson had been coming around every Spring for as long as I could remember. He was a huge, friendly man with shock a of white hair, a kind word, and big, easy smile for everyone he met. Whenever Mr. Robinson's truck came rumbling up the drive, my grandmother would break out the fresh lemonade and some snacks. The visit was more than just a sales call from a vegetable vendor, it was the return of an old friend.

Springtime - the renewal of friendships.

Most appropriately, in the midst of this season of rebirth, we took time to celebrate Easter. This meant going to Fredericksburg to attend church with the rest of the family, and to be a part of one of the most unique Easter traditions to be found anywhere: the Fredericksburg Easter fires.

It is said that the Easter fires began with Indians lighting camp fires in the hills surrounding the town. Although the settlers had signed a peace treaty, parents were concerned that the Indians' fires might frighten the children. The mothers told the children that the Easter bunny was heating large caldrons in which to prepare dyes from the wildflowers and to cook the Easter eggs.

The tradition of the Fredericksburg Easter fires was passed down from one generation to the next and continues to this day as a beautiful and unique observance. The actual fires are still lighted in the hillsides. An Easter pageant is held, complete with children dressed as rabbits, Indians being converted to Christianity, and a re-enactment of the treaty-signing between the Indians and the settlers.

Springtime - the renewal of the spirit.

The renewal of life.

****

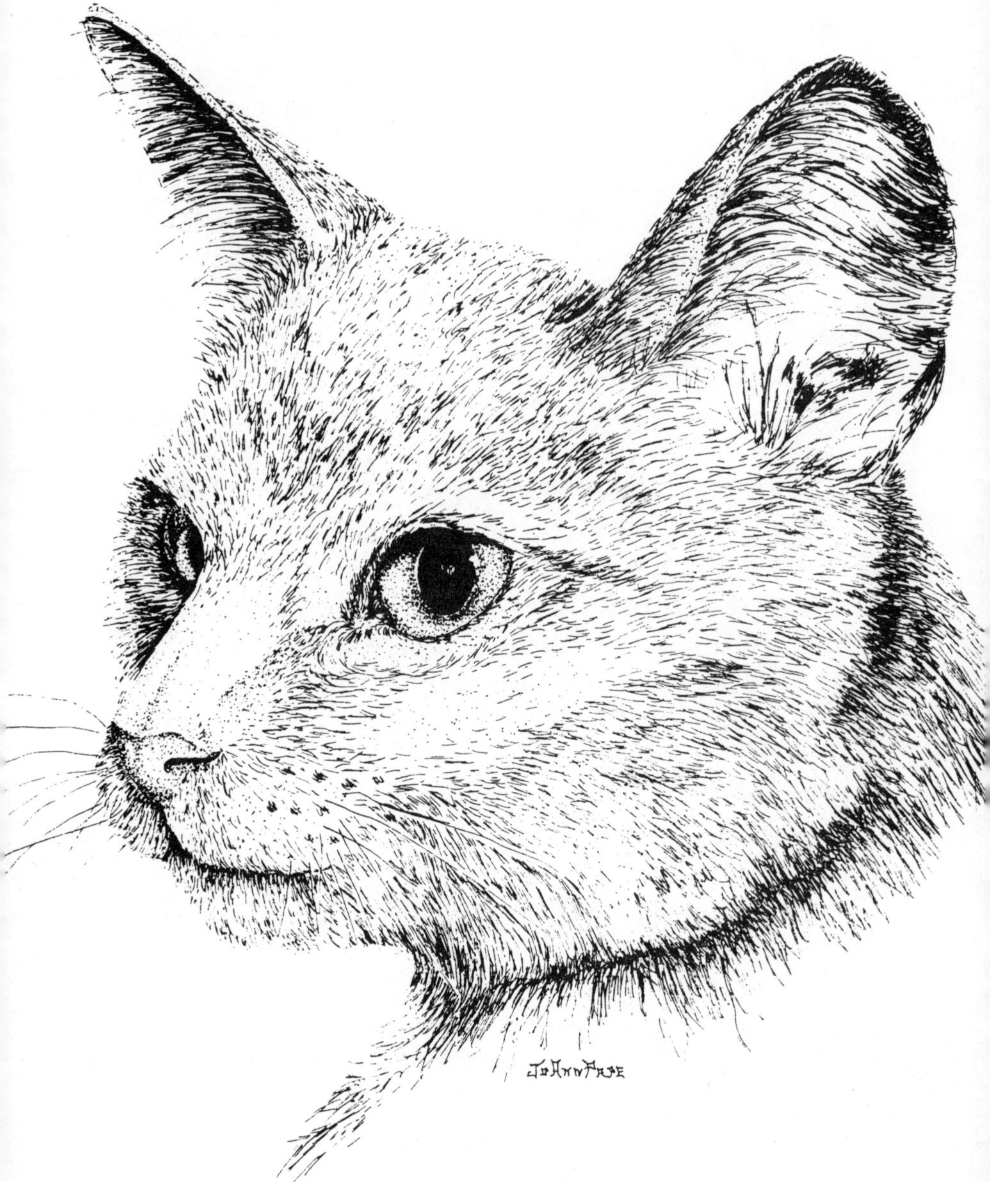

OSCAR

Oscar was probably the oldest cat on earth but, of course, I can't prove that. He was a member of my family before I arrived on the scene, and remained a fixture around the farm until just after I turned seventeen. A lot of cats came and went around our house, but Oscar was always the boss.

Oscar's looks let you know right away that he was the top tomcat in his domain. He was black with a white underside, commanding yellow eyes, and absolutely no tail. No, he didn't lose it; he never had one. Oscar was a Manx, a breed that simply have no tails. It didn't seem to bother him that all the other cats had tails and he did not, it was all just a part of his style.

You could always tell when Oscar found a new girlfriend. A lot of little kittens showed up with half-tails, stump-tails, and no tails. He never actually acknowledged these pretenders to the throne, but the tail situation was a dead giveaway.

Oscar was a farm cat, not a house cat. Most of our cats came and went through the house as they chose. Oscar stayed outside - his choice, not ours. Outside was simply where he felt at home, and the barn was where he worked.

He would spend hours in the barn, usually with my grandfather. He and Opa seemed to have a special relationship, probably because they were a lot alike in temperament. Oscar tolerated us; he loved Opa.

You show a mouse to a lot of cats, and you'll get a lot of different reactions. Some will play; some will run; some will look at you like you're crazy. Oscar was a born mouser.

If you showed a mouse to that old cat, the rodent was quickly dispatched to that great grain bin in the sky. In fact, Oscar would often go to the grain bins in the barn and meow for us to let him in. Once inside, the rodent population was in for the race of their lives.

He also loved to sit under the big pecan tree near the house. We had a wooden picnic table under that tree and Oscar would lay on the table for hours on end, enjoying the shade and serenity.

The mockingbird who nested in the same tree spent an equal number of hours unhappily diving at Oscar's head in an effort to get him to move. Oscar never threatened the nest - his mission in life was mousing - but I suppose the mockingbird was just as obstinate about her tree as Oscar was about his table. Year after year, the bird would defend her tree as Oscar simply ignored the whole thing. He stayed on the table; the bird kept her nest in the tree.

Other than the mockingbird's nesting area, the territory around that tree was Oscar's absolute domain. He slept there, liked to eat there, and tolerated our occasional use of the table provided that we supplied him with a healthy portion of table scraps.

One year my grandmother made the

mistake of hiding an egg under Oscar's table for our annual Easter egg hunt. When we located the egg, Oscar was laid around it. He looked at us as if to say "my table, my egg." No argument - Oscar kept the egg.

As he grew older, Oscar's body waned, but not his spirit. He got to the point where he could no longer jump into the grain bin on his own. He would still sit and meow to be let in. We would lift him into the bin and wait until he was finished with his mouse hunt. The job completed, we would lift him out again. More mice got away, but Oscar was still a mouser and still had his pride.

In his later years, Oscar stayed closer and closer to his picnic table and his favored pecan tree. We wanted to bring him into the house so he could spend his twilight years as a pampered house cat. Oscar wouldn't hear of it. The picnic table was just fine, thank you.

That's where we found him one morning. He had gone to his final rest where he spent so many shady summer afternoons. The great mouser had died, peacefully resting on the picnic table he loved.

Oscar was laid to rest at the base of that tree, right next to his picnic table. And high in the branches of the pecan tree, the mockingbird watched.

Silently.

*****

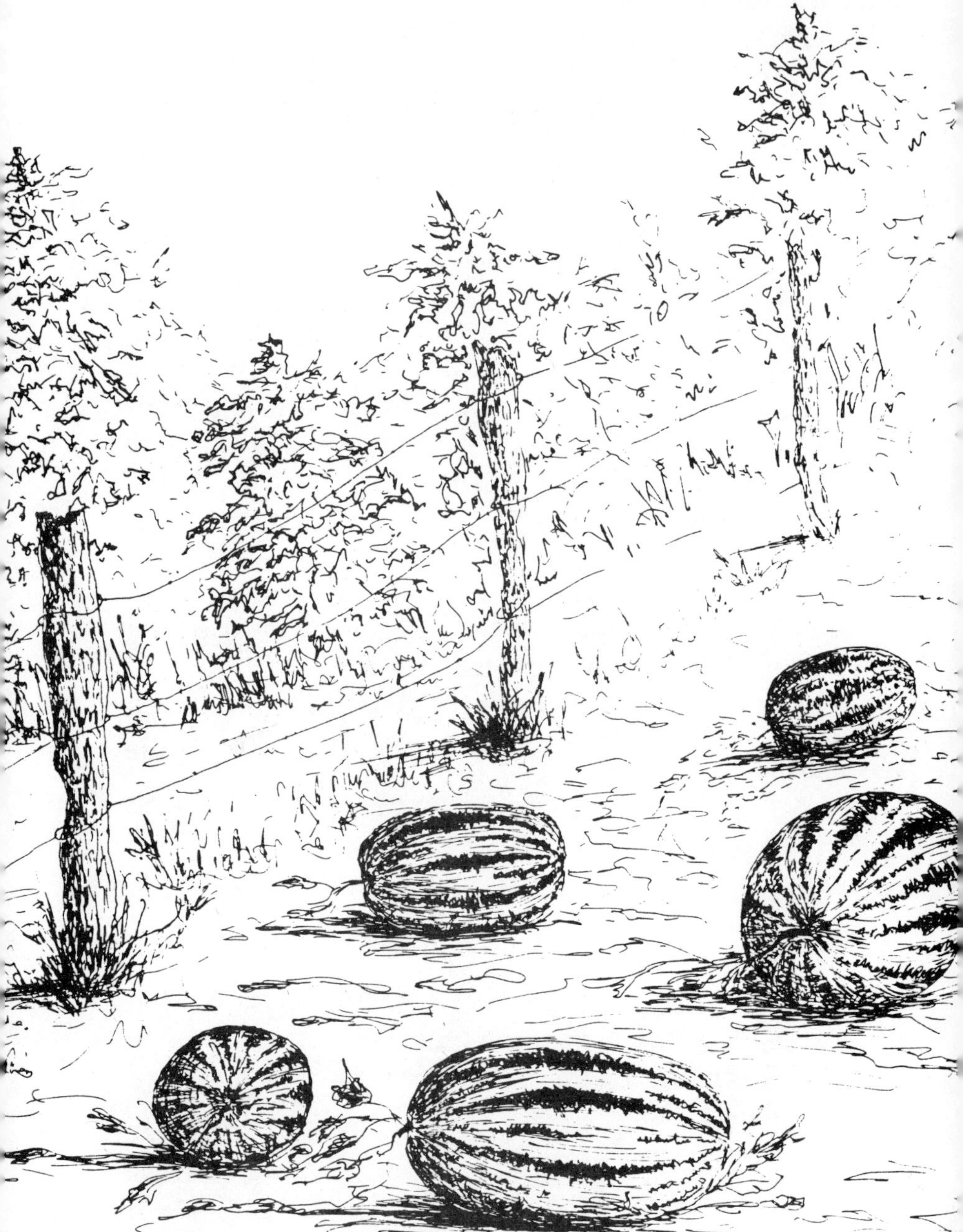

WATERMELON TIME

If there's one thing that just isn't safe around my family, it's a watermelon. If the country's annual watermelon consumption is ever charted by some official tally, I'm absolutely certain that my family alone would equal the amount digested by several Yankee states combined. I can't really offer an explanation other than to say it's hereditary.

I often spent summer days with my great-grandmother - Big Oma as I called her. She would work in the hot sun, armed with a sun bonnet and hoe, to make sure that the watermelons in her small garden received plenty of tender loving care. Peppers, squash, tomatoes, and the rest would be attended in due time, but the needs of the watermelons were always her primary concern.

During those summer days with Big Oma, lunch meant the two of us would share a watermelon, and it was absolutely a sin to walk away until that melon was gone. After a brief rest, Big Oma would be back out in that rocky little garden, guarding her melon crop from potential intruders. We warned her about rattlesnakes in the garden, but Big Oma promptly informed us that she had been dispatching rattlers with her hoe for three-quarters of a century, and she was not going to begin to worry about them now.

The only time I can recall her turning down the offer of a watermelon was one we brought her from Arkansas. That should tell you how prized a watermelon was in my family - we went to the Ozarks on vacation and brought back watermelons for souvenirs.

The only problem was that this particular melon had yellow meat. Big Oma took one look and lectured us on the fact that she had been eating melons for more years than any of us had been around and a proper watermelon had red meat. She then declared the gift some kind of imitation and would have nothing to do with it.

The family tradition of loving watermelons still lives with my grandmother. To this day, Oma is quite content to make a meal of a watermelon, with several slices of butter bread as a side dish.

Since the statute of limitations protects us, I can now confess that we snatched an occasional unguarded melon at Oma's insistence from fields around Stockdale during trips to Corpus Christi. The evidence was usually eaten at a roadside park between the scene of the crime and our destination. In my family, "watermelon munchies" simply cannot be ignored.

During our annual Thanksgiving gathering, we have even been known to hunt down and purchase what must be the last watermelon of the season, regardless of the cost or trouble involved. We then eat it along with the traditional turkey and dressing.

While we may have to eat turkey sandwiches for weeks afterward, there's never any leftover watermelon.

*****

OUTHOUSES

If you lived in the Texas Hill Country during the first half of this century, you probably are well-schooled in the art of using an outhouse - "privy literate," if you will. Unfortunately, outhouses are rapidly going the way of the Texas Horned Toad and nine-pin bowling clubs. They are an endangered species.

Outhouses were once common throughout the Hill Country. The wealthier folks usually had a spacious two-holer with a fine wooden door. The less fortunate usually had to make do with a single-holer with a discarded feed sack for a door. There were even the multi-holed versions serving schools, businesses, and dance halls.

At school, it was typically "girls on one side, boys on the other." The boys who were disciplinary problems usually paid their penance by cleaning out the privy, which could prove to be a challenge if your school had an eight-holer.

In the winter, the privies were cold and uncomfortable; in the summer they were warm and pungent. When seeking relief, you always had to remember that you weren't the only creature who might seek refuge in the little building. A quick inspection for snakes, spiders, wasps, and the like before settling in helped to insure that you wouldn't need to make an unplanned, undignified exit.

Halloween was especially hard on outhouses. Regardless of the "treat" offered, you would often find a "trick" the next morning in the form of your outhouse having been tipped over by a group of roving goblins the night before.

My best boyhood friend, Elroy Dietert, was something of an expert privy-tipper. However, one particularly dark Halloween night, he was tipping over Mr. Krause's outhouse when he lost his footing and fell into the pit. Despite his best effort at cleaning up - which involved jumping into a very chilly Guadalupe River - his acrid aroma gave him away. Elroy's father, an outhouse tipping victim himself, promptly marched the smelly delinquent into the barnyard and scrubbed him down with bleach in an unused horse trough.

Even my high school traditionally topped their annual bonfire with an outhouse. I don't know if this is widely-practiced, but New Braunfels High School just wouldn't have considered it a proper bonfire without a privy on top. With the rapid loss of outhouses, I suppose that this custom, too, will be lost.

We're saving the whales, the rain forests, and the ozone, so why not save the outhouse? They're environmentally sound. They provide a healthy outlet for youthful energy. They can even be a source of community pride when displayed atop a football bonfire.

Besides, can you imagine anyone tying up the toilet facilities for hours at a time in an outhouse?

*****

ABOUT CEDAR-CHOPPERS

On numerous occasions, I have used the term "cedar-chopper" to describe certain natives of the Texas Hill Country. Coming from a long line of cedar-choppers, it only recently dawned on me that there may be some folks who are unfamiliar with this once-plentiful species that inhabited Central Texas.

Cedar-choppers were typically poor, rural Hill Country people who, quite simply, chopped cedar. Not for fun, not for exercise, and not out of an inherent dislike for cedar trees. They chopped cedar to make a living.

At one time, cedar was used in the building of virtually every kind of structure in the Hill Country, from homes to chicken coops to outhouses. The better pieces were hewn for planks of lumber, while the smaller trunks and limbs were used for fence posts.

For the sake of satisfying the purists, what we in the Hill Country call cedar is actually Mexican Juniper. It is also known as Juniper Cedar. The term cedar is so prevalent, however, that it has virtually replaced the proper name. Besides, it just wouldn't sound right calling my ancestors "juniper choppers".

It goes without saying that cedar chopping was neither pleasant nor particularly profitable. It was said that you could tell an "affluent" chopper by the fact that he had a double-bit chopping axe, smoked ready-rolled cigarettes, and had a door on his outhouse.

Cedar-choppers were usually the poorest of the poor. Most eked out a bare existence, living in tents back in the hills while chopping and selling the wood. The cedar was sold to cedar yards that were once plentiful throughout the area. When the cedar supply was exhausted, the choppers simply packed their tent and meager belongings, and moved on.

Although the term cedar-chopper was often used as a term of derision, most cedar-choppers were proud and fiercely independent. Many, quite literally, lived off the land. The backwoods provided a home; the cedar provided a small income; deer, rabbit, squirrel, and possum provided food.

My uncle Adolph Pfeuffer was just such a person. In his younger days, Adolph chopped cedar to make enough money to buy a small homestead. By living off the land and saving the money he made selling cedar, he was able to buy a small plot of land to farm and build a cabin for his family.

Even after Adolph gave up cedar chopping for farming, he managed to make a little extra "beer-drinking money" by selling kindling and his own version of homemade cedar charcoal. He came upon these ideas because of his inherently-frugal German nature.

As he chopped wood for the fireplace, Adolph couldn't help thinking about all of the tiny chips of cedar that were too small for the wood pile. Typically, he would gather them in a large pile and use these small pieces for kindling to start a fire. Unfortunately, there was always more kindling than he needed, and the pile grew larger and larger.

Not one to tolerate waste, Adolph came up with a profitable idea. If he needed kindling to start a fire, so did the people in town. The town folks, however, didn't cut their own wood; they bought it from cedar-choppers. If they were willing to buy wood, why not kindling?

The next Saturday, Adolph filled his old feed sacks full of kindling wood, loaded them onto the mule cart, and headed for town. Finding a spot at the marketplatz (market plaza) alongside the farmers selling their vegetables, the cedar-chip entrepreneur quickly sold out of the kindling at 15-cents a bag.

Realizing that he had a good thing going, Adolph went one step further. He gathered all of the cedar chips that were too large for kindling but not big enough for other uses, dug a large pit, and threw the excess cedar inside. He then wet everything down, covered it with dirt and left it. Three to four weeks later, the end result was homemade charcoal.

For many years thereafter, before daybreak every Saturday, Uncle Adolph would load his sacks of kindling and homemade charcoal into the wagon and head for town to get a good spot at the marketplatz. He even gained customers along the way where he could stop and make home deliveries. Adolph was, quite possibly, the first door-to-door cedar-chopper/charcoal salesman in Texas.

There are only a few cedar-choppers left

in Texas today and they are, sadly, a vanishing breed. The double-bit axe has been replaced with a chainsaw, the mule cart by a flatbed truck, and crews of cedar-choppers by bulldozers.

Uncle Adolph used to say that cutting cedar was something that was "in your blood". Maybe that's why I love to walk through the cedar-covered hillsides, smelling that special "cedar smell" in the cool morning air.

Maybe, too, that's why my wife never gets me that chainsaw I ask for every Christmas.

*****

THE KING OF WESTERN SWING

There is no music more "Texas" than western swing. Today, there are only a few artists that still play and record classic western swing numbers. Maybe so few try because it's hard to compete against the standard set by the greatest western swing band ever - Bob Wills and the Texas Playboys.

I was lucky enough to see Bob Wills and the Texas Playboys at their last public performance. It was a benefit in San Antonio to raise money for Wills' medical expenses. It was also one of life's special moments - the opportunity to see a living legend, in fact a group of living legends, making the music that made them famous.

The Texas Playboys stopped performing regularly in the 1960's. In 1969, Wills had a stroke that paralyzed his right side. He would be confined to a wheelchair for the rest of his life, never again to play the legendary Bob Wills fiddle.

Bob Wills had forever put San Antonio on the musical map with his classic rendition of "San Antonio Rose". In return, the people of San Antonio never forgot Bob or his music. As the bills for his medical and therapy expenses mounted, San Antonio decided to give Bob Wills a special birthday party. The event would also raise money to, in some small way, repay him for all of the pleasure he had given to others.

The event was held at the Municipal Auditorium on March 6, 1973, Bob's 68th birthday. It brought the Texas Playboys back together for the first time in many years. Because of Bob's frail health, it was decided that his brother, Johnny Lee Wills, would fill in for Bob as the band recreated the sound that made them famous.

On the night of the concert, the crowd at the auditorium was tremendous. People in their seventies waited anxiously alongside youngsters in their teens. There was some concern over whether Bob's health would even permit him to appear on stage, but no one seemed concerned. The chance to hear the original western swing sound, with only the possibility of just a glimpse of the King of Western Swing, would make it all worthwhile.

As with any good show, there needed to be an opening act. The question was, who do you get to open for living legends like Bob Wills and the Texas Playboys? The answer - another country music legend.

America's most beloved cowboy, Tex Ritter, had learned of the benefit and offered to donate his time to open the show. Under most circumstances, the chance to see Tex Ritter would alone be worth the price of a ticket.

As the time arrived for the Texas Playboys to begin, the crowd fell absolutely silent. The curtain went up with the stage still in darkness - and then the announcement:

"Ladies and gentlemen, Bob Wills and the Texas Playboys!" The applause was deafening.

As the first strains of "San Antonio Rose" filled the auditorium, the lights came up to reveal Bob Wills, from his wheelchair, leading the Texas Playboys. The cheering crowd completely drowned out the first stanza of the song they all came to hear.

For the next forty minutes, Bob Wills led the Texas Playboys through some of their most famous numbers. The only difference was the wheelchair. The band received seven standing ovations - one for every song they performed.

As steel guitarist Leon McAuliffe hit the intro to his famous "Steel Guitar Rag", Wills uttered his legendary phrase, "Aah ha, take it away, Leon." There wasn't a dry eye in the house. A huge, burly man with long sideburns and black cowboy hat was standing next to me; tears were streaming down his cheeks.

The show was supposed to end with Bob and the band remaining on stage as Tompall and the Glaser Brothers sang "Faded Love" as a tribute. It was a moving number, but when the Glasers were finished, Bob Wills wasn't. He called Leon McAuliffe over. Bob wanted to do "That's What I Like About the South."

The Texas Playboys played the song. Bob Wills was still their leader, and they would play as long as he wanted them to.

It was a night of magic but, like all things, the gathering of legends had to come to an end. Later that year, they would all reunite one last time in a recording studio. They would spend several days re-recording their legendary music for one last album. Not long after that, Bob Wills was gone.

The benefit that night in San Antonio raised over $12,000 but, as usual, Bob Wills gave much more than he received. We gave him a grand birthday party. He gave us a memory that will last forever.

*****

BELLY-UP TO THE WORM BAR

I opened the Sunday newspaper a few weeks back to find a full-color ad from a sporting goods store encouraging customers to "Visit Texas' Finest Worm Bar - The Largest in the State". The ad went on to offer a "gigantic assortment of worms" including shrimptails, shad, gitzits, ringworms, and grubs, all for only 8 cents apiece.

I knew what a bar was, having patronized such an establishment once or twice in my life. I also am familiar with salad bars, potato bars, and dessert bars. But a worm bar? My first thought was that the health-food fanatics had gone too far this time.

I just wasn't sure what to make of the whole situation, so I asked my wife. She was born and raised in Louisiana - a state where people routinely eat what we Texans consider bait. She would know the answer.

You don't eat them," my wife explained patiently, "they're for fishermen."

"What ever happened to live worms?" I asked. "And crickets? When I was a kid, all we ever used were worms and crickets on the end of a cane pole."

She gave me one of those "once a cedar-chopper, always a cedar-chopper" looks.

"You haven't been fishing in years," she pointed out. "People don't dig up a bucket of worms and cut a cane pole anymore. They buy artificial lures and plastic worms."

"Besides," she reminded me, "the last time you went fishing the only thing you hooked was a wasp nest. You got stung, turned over the boat, cussed for an hour straight, and swore you'd never go fishing again."

She was, of course, right. I pulled out my old fishing license and examined the date. It had expired when John Connally was still governor, and when savings and loans were considered safe places to keep your money. That's a long time ago.

I thought back to those lazy summer days when I went fishing with Opa. We would take our cane poles, dig up some worms, and sit on the side of a stock tank waiting for a small bass or perch to bite. I also wondered what ever became of Mr. Hasse, the Hill Country worm rancher.

Elmer Hasse's Worm Ranch supplied those little cardboard boxes filled with dirt and live worms to all of the bait stands and ice houses around Canyon Lake. He was always quick to correct someone who mistakenly called his operation a "worm farm".

"It's not a farm," Elmer would curtly reply. "A farm grows crops. These worms are living stock, just like cattle. You wouldn't call the King Ranch a cow farm, would you?"

Elmer's "ranch" was located in his back yard. He had row upon row of large wooden boxes, filled with moist dirt and humus. He carefully tended his stock, making certain that the soil always had just enough moisture and shade. He even developed his own "secret-formula worm food" to help his slithering herd grow and prosper.

I got to know about Elmer's operation by working for him. Whenever the time came to "round up" the worms and package them for sale, he would hire some of the neighborhood kids to help.

Before starting, he would carefully instruct us on how much soil and humus to put in each little container. He would then show us precisely how large each worm should be. He reminded us that he had to protect his reputation for selling only the finest and largest bait worms in Central Texas.

Finally, and most importantly, Elmer carefully explained exactly how many worms were to go into each container. Too few worms meant dissatisfied customers. Too many worms cut into his profit.

We were paid between 50 cents and a dollar, depending on how many containers we filled and how many mistakes were caught. A stickler for quality-control, Elmer made spot checks on the size and number of worms we were packaging. Too many mistakes and your pay was cut by twenty-five cents.

A few years ago, after decades of worm ranching, Elmer retired. He decided to give up the bait business because of advancing age and a declining market.

"I'm getting too old to make those weekly rounds of every little bait shop," Elmer told his friends. "Besides, folks today like those artificial lures, expensive rods and reels, and fishing from a fancy bass boat. That kind of fisherman just doesn't have any use for live worms."

Elmer was right. Today's fishermen are far too sophisticated to be caught with a cane pole, a cork, and a worm on the end of a hook.

I imagine that the fish are a lot more sophisticated, too. After all, what self-respecting bass would want to hit on a live worm when they could have for a genuine plastic worm bought at "Texas' Finest Worm Bar"?

*****

GOLD IN THEM THAR HILLS?

The Hill Country is full of legend and lore about hidden and lost treasures. Although these legends have never been proven, the stories persist from one generation to the next.

One of the most durable legends involves the lost San Saba, or Bowie, mine. This tale tells of a lost silver mine somewhere near present-day Menard. A rich vein of silver was supposedly discovered by Spanish explorers in the 18th century after they heard Indian legends about a rumored Cerro de la Plata (Silver Hill). Mining operations were reportedly conducted by the Spaniards until the late 1700's when repeated attacks from the Comanches forced them to abandon the area.

The legend of the Hill of Silver was subsequently told throughout Texas and eventually caught the ear of the newly-arrived Jim Bowie. In an effort to learn more about the legendary treasure, Bowie shrewdly cultivated the friendship of the Lipan Indian Chief Xolic by presenting him with a silver-plated rifle. In return, Xolic made Bowie a blood brother and permitted him to live among the tribe.

Having won the confidence of the Lipans, Bowie learned the location of the lost silver mine. Astounded by the size of the Indian treasure, he immediately returned to San Antonio to recruit help to capture the mine. He rounded up ten volunteers, including his brother Rezin P. Bowie, and set out to seize the silver.

At sunrise on November 21, 1831, the Bowie party was attacked along Calf Creek in present-day McCulloch County by a party of more than 150 Indians. A fierce battle ensued which left one Texan dead and two wounded. The Indians fared much worse with a reported 80 killed; however, Bowie was driven back to San Antonio. It is believed that this was Bowie's last attempt to claim the mine, although it was rumored that he was planning another expedition as late as three months before he was killed in the Alamo.

In recent times, an individual in Kansas claimed to have a map, taken from Bowie's body by a Mexican officer immediately after the fall of the Alamo, which gave directions to the lost mine. Despite this claim of a map, the mine, if it actually exists, has never been found.

Stories of lost treasure are just as prevalent in the eastern portion of the Hill Country. Generations of fortune hunters have searched along the lakes of Bell, Falls, and Williamson Counties for the lost Steinheimer treasure. A German immigrant, Karl Steinheimer, is alleged to have amassed a fortune through dealings with pirates and, as the legend goes, buried the booty in a cave near a small lake in this area. As with the Bowie mine, claims of maps to the Steinheimer treasure have surfaced from time to time, but none of the fortune has ever been found.

Lockhart, too, has its story of lost treasure. Before the Civil War, a raiding party of Indians attacked and looted Lockhart, loading a treasure of silver onto a wagon. As the settlers gathered to re-take the town, the Indians abducted a woman, fleeing with her and the wagon load of silver.

At Clear Fork Creek, about two miles west of town, the Indians apparently realized that they could not outrun the settlers, so the treasure was thrown into the creek. The settlers did eventually overtake the Indians about 8 miles south of town, but the woman hostage was killed.

That this event actually occurred can be confirmed by the fact that the grave of the slain woman can still be viewed on the Prairie Lea-Lockhart road, about a mile and a half south of town. The silver, however, was never recovered. Many still say that a fortune in silver lies buried beneath a hundred-years' worth of silt in Clear Fork Creek.

These are just a few of the lost treasure stories that abound in the Texas Hill Country. While the histories of some of these stories may be somewhat doubtful, the legends are assured by generations of tales of lost wealth. These legends, true or not, are a part of the heritage of the Hill Country - waiting for the next generation of explorers.

*****

BODO SCHWAMKRUG'S IN LOVE

Everyone has a first love. In the case of Bodo Schwamkrug, that love blossomed during his freshman year in high school. He was eighteen at the time.

Bodo, you see, was what we used to call "a little slow". Actually, that's what his mother called him; we kids called him Dodo and we were his friends.

Even his teachers called him Dodo. He was the only student in the history of New Braunfels

High School to fail study hall. The standing joke was that Dodo never showed up because study hall was always held in room 22 and Dodo couldn't count past eleventeen.

Bodo was easy to spot in a crowd. He was just over six-feet tall with an unruly shock of red hair. In warm weather, he wore a white tee-shirt and overalls with a red bandana hanging out of his right rear pocket. In cold weather, he wore a blue flannel shirt and overalls with a red bandana hanging out of his right rear pocket.

Despite his intellectual and apparel shortcomings, Dodo was always my friend. For one thing, he was a German farm kid like me. In high school circles, German farm kids ranked at the bottom of the social barrel - right there with the goofy foreign-exchange student who never quite mastered the art of zipping his pants.

Also, as I mentioned, he was big. The fact that he was the same age as the graduating seniors had a lot to do with it, but regardless of the reason, Dodo's size helped us avoid any kind of trouble. Even the teachers thought twice before correcting some indiscretion if Dodo was involved.

Our freshman year rocked along quietly with Dodo as our mentor. He protected us and helped us along. After all, he knew the ropes - it was his third time as a freshman. Everything was right with the world. Everything, that is, until Dodo fell in love.

Most of our little circle had experienced at least one teenage romance by this time, so it shouldn't have come as a surprise to us that, at age eighteen, Bodo Schwamkrug discovered girls. But when Dodo met Hilda "the Javelina" Schneider, it was an unexpected match made in heaven.

The Javelina was perfect for Dodo. She was best known as the star of the school's wrestling team - and we didn't have a girl's team. She played tuba in the school band and drove a flatbed truck.

Hilda was also a highly sought-after baby-sitter. Parents trusted her, mostly because they figured there was no way she would attract boys while baby-sitting. It was rumored that the kids never got into any trouble because they spent the entire time hiding in fright from her. There was even a story that one terrified child refused to come out from under his bed for three days after Hilda was gone.

We realized that something was up between Dodo and the Javelina when they started walking together between classes. He was carrying her books; she was carrying his plug of chewing tobacco.

"Hey, Dodo, where you been?" I called out.

He shot me a look that would kill, excused himself from his lady-love, and dragged me by my collar into the boy's room.

"Knock off the 'Dodo' stuff around Hilda," he told me in no uncertain terms. "It's Bodo in front of my girlfriend."

"You mean you and the Jave...uh, I mean, Hilda are, uh, well, uh, dating?"

"Yeah," he answered. "She's pretty and

smart, and she really likes me. Isn't she wonderful?"

"Uh, well, uh, you know, I hear she plays a really great tuba," I babbled, groping for something nice to say. "And she doesn't sweat much for a big girl."

Oops.

"Yeah," Bodo agreed. "You're right, she doesn't."

Thank goodness Bodo was easily impressed by a compliment.

Although we stayed good friends, things were never quite the same after Bodo met Hilda. They continued to date throughout high school. In her case that was three more years; in his case it was five.

After high school, they married. Bodo started a business driving a dump truck. Hilda opened a popular day-care center. The children are said to be very well-behaved, but immensely relieved to get home.

I ran into Bodo recently as he was coming out of a downtown bank.

"Don't have time to talk," he told me as he jumped into his new Lincoln Continental. "I'm on my way to see my broker. I've got $400,000 to get into a tax shelter before the taxes eat me up. See you soon."

As he drove off, I read the personalized license plate on the back of his Lincoln:

"DODO."

*****

UNCLE HERBERT'S STILL

Uncle Herbert was a moonshiner. But if you have images of Burt Reynolds in "White Lightning" or Robert Mitchum in "Thunder Road," you've got the wrong idea. To put it kindly, Uncle Herbert had what you might call an over-appreciation for adult beverages and, being a frugal German, simply felt it was far less expensive and more expedient to make your own.

Herbert's still was hidden in the cedar brush near Bear Creek between Sattler and Startzville in Comal County. From this hallowed, hidden spot, he distilled and bottled his cedar-chopper jet fuel for fun and profit. While the still was originally built for personal use, the old moonrunner quickly became a whiskey entrepreneur as the reputation of his brew spread throughout the hills.

Never one to miss the chance at a quick buck, Herbert began to bottle his hootch and sell whatever he couldn't drink. Selling the stuff for a dollar a gallon to his friends and neighbors, Herbert's booze developed a strong following among the hill folks.

As his customers would tell you, the first couple of swigs tasted a little rough but, after that, it tasted as smooth as the best store-bought booze. The popular theory was that the first sip deadened the taste buds to the point that kerosene would taste smooth. Despite these minor shortcomings, Herbert's business grew steadily.

As Herbert's home-brew became more popular, he started selling it by the fruit jar for a quarter apiece at dances. From Fischer Store to Hancock, Smithson's Valley to Bergheim, Herbert visited dancehalls to peddle his brew to the weekend polka patrons. It was said that Herbert's moonshine was as popular as the "Beer Barrel Polka", and no dance was complete without several rounds of both.

Herbert and his German joy-juice enlivened parties throughout the countryside until the end of the still came at the hands of Mother

Nature. It seems that the still had been built a little too close to the creek. As occasionally happens in the Hill Country, a heavy rain brought the normally-placid stream to floodstage, and the roaring waters quickly wiped out the prosperous backwoods brewery.

Herbert never rebuilt the still, and the popular story was that the loss of the still seemed to have broken the old moonrunner's desire to brew his illegal grog. More probably, he heard that the Sheriff had gotten wind of the still after hearing complaints from the wives of German farmers who were still too drunk to work on Monday morning.

The loss of the still was felt for weeks after the flood. The old men who sat around the Startzville store told stories about finding tipsy cattle and goats down along Bear Creek. And the dances were never as much fun as when the life of the party came in a fruit jar.

*****

NIGHT OF THE KILLING WATERS

Not long ago, a real estate agent was showing my wife and I a piece of Hill Country property. It was a beautiful, peaceful setting beneath huge oak trees along the Guadalupe River.

"Right over there," the agent said as he pointed to a spot between several large trees, "would be the perfect place to build a home. Your back yard would run right up to the edge of the river."

"What about floods?" I asked.

The agent, obviously a newcomer to the Hill Country, looked at me like I had a screw loose.

"I can't imagine what you'd have to worry about," he said. "Canyon Dam is only about 15 miles upstream, and it would stop any flood waters. I can't even tell you how long it's been since this area flooded."

"I can," I told him, "May 11, 1972."

The night of May 11 and 12, 1972, is forever imprinted in my memory. It was a night when over 10 inches of rain fell within a two-hour period between New Braunfels and Canyon Dam. It became known as the Night of the Killing Waters.

As the torrents of rain fell across the hillsides, the watersheds drained the rainfall into the tributaries of the Guadalupe and Comal Rivers. The tranquil, clear waters that give life to the surrounding Hill Country quickly became enraged torrents of destruction, devastating everything in their path.

Plunging downstream into New Braunfels in two separate walls of water, the flood took fifteen lives and left almost $20 million of damage in its wake. Screams of terror filled the night air, adding to the horror of the destruction.

I was trying to make it home during the height of the downpour, when I stopped to help my friend, Elroy Dietert, whose car had flooded out on a street near Landa Park. After we got Elroy's car out of the water, he asked me to stay with it while he went to check on some other people who were also stranded nearby.

Almost as soon as Elroy disappeared into the rainy darkness, I began to hear a strange, low roar in the distance. The roar grew louder, and before I could comprehend what was happening, a surging wall of water was upon me. I grabbed the door of Elroy's car and held on for dear life.

The force of the water carried the car well into the park, finally lodging it against a group of trees. Somehow, the water washed Elroy back to the same area, leaving us both clinging to the same tree against the flood's torrent.

As we held fast to the tree, we were battered by an assortment of debris being washed downstream. At one point, we could hear a voice screaming for help in the distance. We shouted back, but there was little else we could do. Eventually, the voice disappeared into the darkness.

After what seemed an eternity, the ferocity of the flood subsided a bit, allowing us the chance to climb higher into the tree. We could hear helicopters overhead, but we knew that the same trees that gave us refuge would prevent us from being seen from the air. The only thing we could do was wait.

Shortly after daybreak, a National Guard rescue party found us. We were wet, exhausted, and battered - but extremely fortunate to be alive.

Only after our rescue did we begin to realize how widespread the destruction was. Lives were certainly lost, but no one yet knew how many. Entire neighborhoods were gone, leaving hundreds homeless.

As we were driven to the nearest shelter, we could see the destruction firsthand. Only foundations remained where the day before beautiful brick homes stood. Other homes were moved hundreds of feet. Cars were tossed about like toys. Debris filled the streets.

In the days after the flood, Elroy and I, like most everyone else, worked with a search party looking for victims. Our group found two - a young mother and her year-old son. We found their bodies buried beneath a pile of rubble downstream from Landa Park.

We later learned that the lady had carried her baby to the roof of their home to escape the flood waters. The second wave of water washed them both to their death. They would have floated through the park where Elroy and I were clinging to the tree. We both couldn't help but wonder if her's was the voice we heard crying for help in the middle of the night.

Neither Elroy or I knew the victims whose bodies we recovered, but we both went to their funeral. We didn't know why; it just seemed like the right thing to do. Their names were Shirley and Brian Ray Moos.

Twenty years ago, people believed that they had tamed the river. It had become something of a benign tourist attraction.

It was nothing more than a prestigious amenity for expensive housing developments. People could have the river in their backyards, just like a pet dog. They had lost respect for the destruction Mother Nature could unleash through the Hill Country's rivers and streams.

It seems like we have, again, lost that respect for the destructive potential of the river. Time has passed, and the dead are long-buried. Some have forgotten. Others don't think it can ever happen again.

I believe that we all have a very personal Hell. Mine is the Night of the Killing Waters. I won't forget.

*****

SUMMER IN THE HILL COUNTRY

*****

SKY KING AND ME

"From out of the clear blue of the western sky - it's Sky King!"

With those words, Sky King would fly his trusty airplane, the Songbird, across the Saturday-morning television skies to the delight of children viewers. Growing up in the 1950's, a kid could follow the exploits of all kinds of heroes - Roy Rogers, Davy Crockett, Superman, the Lone Ranger and, of course, Sky King.

At Lamar Elementary School, you could always tell a boy's personal favorite. The Davy Crockett guys showed up in coon-skin caps. The Superman fans were the ones who tried flying off of the swings on the playground. Roy Rogers disciples came to school wearing cowboy hats with strings under the chin and toy six-shooters that were confiscated by the teachers the minute they hit the school yard. Followers of the Lone Ranger looked a lot like the Roy Rogers kids except they had masks and tried to cultivate other kids to follow them around, grunt, and say "Kemosabe" a lot.

Those hearty few who didn't fall into one of the above categories were usually fans of Sky

King. Unfortunately, Sky King just didn't lend himself to the sort of impersonation that the other heroes generated.

He didn't have super powers; he didn't live in the old west; he didn't dress funny; he didn't always carry a gun. He was your run-of-the-mill millionaire rancher dedicated to fighting crooks in Arizona (or somewhere out West - we were never absolutely sure) by flying them down in his Twin Cessna. Most importantly, he was our number-one good-guy hero.

Those of us who lived from one Saturday to the next to watch Sky King's adventures endured the ridicule of others. Kids with Superman tee-shirts, Roy Rogers six-shooters, Lone Ranger masks, and genuine imitation dead raccoons on their heads were the first to taunt us about our hero's lack of color.

"Just a rich guy who flies an airplane," they would tell us. "You can't even buy a Sky King lunch pail."

With the stoic dignity of Sky King himself, we endured these taunts knowing that, someday, our loyalty would be rewarded and our hero would avenge us. Like any good hero, he came to our rescue.

The first poster appeared in the front window of the Ol' Bossy Dairy on a Monday afternoon. The dairy would open a new store in two weeks. There would be free ice cream and balloons. Sky King would appear.

Sky King would appear! In only two weeks! Our hero, obviously aware of our unflagging loyalty, was coming to the Hill Country to see us.

The next two weeks were both the longest and sweetest of my life. Those who had ridiculed our hero for so long were silent. They had been ranked and they knew it. They could have their silly little souvenirs - we had Sky King in person.

When the fateful Saturday came, I was, of course, among the seething, scratching, sweating crowd of youngsters gathered in the parking lot, waiting for the chance to meet our television hero. The wait was interminable. Speeches were made; pictures were taken; ribbons were cut - all adult stuff.

Finally, he appeared. Sky King, resplendent in his western-cut suit, cowboy hat, and string tie, appeared before the worshipping throngs of little cedar-choppers. We were herded into a line and all given photos of Sky to be autographed.

As I reached the front of the line, he broadly grinned at me.

"What's your name, young man?" he asked.

Name? Name?? My mind was blank! Wait a minute, I knew my name when I got here.

"John," I finally babbled.

"Well, John, I'm Sky King. I'm pleased to meet you."

I stood there - dumbstruck.

"Would you like me to autograph that for you?" he asked, gesturing at the photo.

"Uh...uh...uh...," I promptly replied.

"I'm glad to have met you, John," he said as he signed the photo. "Now remember to listen to your parents and drink all of your Ol' Bossy milk."

As the fog lifted from my brain, I became

aware of someone shoving an ice cream cone and balloon into my hand. My meeting with Sky King was over, but clutched in the strongest death-grip a six-year-old could muster was my autographed photo of Sky King. My proof to the world that I had met my hero.

Sky King's gone now, but I still have that autographed photo as one of my most treasured momentos. Todays' kids are enthralled by strange creatures like Teenage Mutant Ninja Turtles and Hulk Hogan, and probably would not be impressed with the likes of a Sky King.

But every now and again, on a Saturday morning, Sky King still flies the Songbird across the black and white skies of cable television. And I, with my autographed picture, can be six-years old again.

*****

MR. EBELL'S CAVE

One sunny autumn afternoon, while driving northeast out of Boerne I noticed a small, undistinguished sign that said simply "Cave Without A Name" and an arrow pointing down a little country lane.

"Cave Without A Name?" I thought to myself. A distant memory was telling me that I had heard of this place before. I just couldn't place it. I stopped on the roadside, studied the simple sign, and pondered.

Finally, it came to me - a faded, cracked old photograph, at least fifty years old, from the family album. My great-grandmother, grandmother, uncle, and father (no more than 10 years old) standing in front of a stone grotto entrance. Handwritten across the border of the old photo: "We all visit Cave Without A Name."

Curiosity overwhelmed me, even to the point of overcoming my deathly fear of dark, threatening places (such as caves, elevators, and dentist's offices). I had to see this place.

After several miles, the paved lane became a gravel road. A half-mile or so beyond that I encountered a small, hand-lettered sign: "Cave Information at Trailer," referring to a neatly-kept mobile home alongside the road.

My knock on the door was greeted by Mr. Ebell who, with his wife, owns and operates Cave Without A Name.

"Interested in a cave tour?" he asked. "OK, drive on down the road about a hundred yards and you'll see the entrance. I'll get the keys and meet you there."

Cave Without A Name is not your typical tourist attraction. You won't see Burma Shave-style signs every mile along the highway. They don't have a souvenir shop, snack bar, or kiddie rides. This is a cave that is lovingly cared for by a man who knows it's every secret, and willingly shares his knowledge with those who will take the time to look, listen, and learn.

Mr. Ebell begins his lesson even before the gate leading into the cave is opened. Speaking with an ever-so-slight German accent, my host began to tell me the history of Cave Without a Name. No rehearsed speech is given; everything comes from years of intimate knowledge of the cave. This is no tour; this is a lesson from the heart.

Cave Without a Name opened in 1939, I was told, becoming one of the first caves to be opened for public tours. It was apparently not long after that opening that my family visited and took the group photo.

"There was a contest to pick a name for the cave." Mr. Ebell explained. "One young boy went through the cave and said that it was just too pretty to name. Ever since then, it's been called Cave Without A Name."

As we descended the narrow, winding stairs into the cave below, Mr. Ebell called my attention to the soot marks on the walls. It seems that an enterprising moonshiner had once stumbled into the cave. Recognizing the value of such concealment, he used it as a hiding place to operate his still in order to avoid detection by the local sheriff. My Uncle Herbert, the family moonshiner, would have been proud of such ingenuity.

Once inside the cave proper, my host led me from room to room, describing all of the processes of nature at work inside the cavern. From stalagmites to stalactites, fried eggs to soda straws, Mr. Ebell provided me with information that comes only from a lifetime of knowledge and experience. For the next hour or so, I listened and learned as we were surrounded by the beauty and majesty of mother nature beneath the world as we know it.

I was disappointed as we began our ascent out of Mr. Ebell's subterranean province. Not disappointed in what I had seen and experienced, but disappointed that my time in the cave was over. I was also disappointed that I didn't have more time to spend with this fine old gentleman and his wealth of knowledge.

There are many caves throughout the Hill Country. Some may be bigger; some may have picnic parks and camping spaces; some will sell you tee-shirts that will proclaim to the world where you've been; all are probably easier to get to.

But at Cave Without A Name you will get something special from Mr. Ebell - the wisdom, the knowledge, and the pride that all come with years of caring for a special part of the Hill Country.

*****

A GOLF BET WITH GOD

They say the first step to dealing with a problem is to admit that you have a problem. OK, here goes: I have a problem with golf. I love playing golf, but I'm simply no good at it.

I've taken lessons, watched Lee Trevino videotapes, and read Jack Nicklaus' book. Despite it all, I still have a handicap somewhere just short of infinity and am more dangerous on a golf course than a lightning storm. I refuse to use golf balls with my name imprinted on them because I'm afraid they could be used as evidence against me.

JoAnn, my wife and chief critic, attributes these problems to my heritage.

"You hit the ball like you're digging post holes," she observed. "You putt like you're weeding a garden, and you swear like a longshoreman when you miss a shot. You even drive the golf cart like it's a tractor. You've just got cedar-chopper written all over you."

In spite of these shortcomings, I've played golf, or at least tried to, at a number of exclusive clubs and resorts. Despite my best efforts to fit in, I've often looked more like a hound dog at a cotillion than Arnold Palmer at Pebble Beach.

Some time ago, I had the opportunity to play golf at the Pedernales Country Club outside of Austin. That's the golf course that Willie Nelson once owned before the IRS seized it for back taxes. Before the club became a government asset, Willie often invited his famous friends to join him for a round of golf at his personal golf course.

I arrived at mid-morning and checked in at the pro shop. The walls were lined with gold records and photos of Willie and many of his famous guests.

The photos included Willie and other country music greats such as Kris Kristofferson and Waylon Jennings. Golf legend Arnold Palmer was pictured, as was the twosome of former Dallas Cowboy coach Tom Landry and football great Earl Campbell. Other photos included actors, singers, politicians, and even one ex-President of the United States.

Seeing all of this, I began wondering just what I'd gotten myself into. How could I get through this without humiliation, especially on a golf course where the rich and famous play?

"Seems like quite a few famous folks have played here," I remarked to the pro-shop attendant.

"Yeah, Willie invites a lot of his friends to play," came the reply. "We're kind of isolated out here, so they like to drop by for a quiet round from time to time."

"Anyone famous out there today?" I asked.

"Well, I'm not supposed to tell anyone, but there's a big-time country singer playing a round with a senator," the attendant told me. "They teed off about ten minutes ago. They're just ahead of you, so try not to get too close. The bodyguards get nervous."

"You mean the senator has bodyguards?"

"Of course not. The bodyguards are for the singer. One of his ex-wives is trying to serve him with court papers."

As I stood on the first tee, I visualized the next day's headline: "Famous People Killed on Willie Nelson's Golf Course - Errant Golf Ball From Golfing Cedar-Chopper Blamed". Worse yet, what if I accidentally hit a shot too close to the singer/senator pair? What would the bodyguards do to me? I immediately bargained with God.

"Please let me get through this without hurting anybody," I prayed aloud. "If I do, please don't let it be anyone important. I'll go back to church. I'll even put some money in the plate."

God had no immediate reply.

I reminded God about my perfect attendance pin from third-grade Sunday School class.

God still offered no reply.

Seeing no other option, I decided to take my chances and hit the ball. My first shot sailed gracefully skyward and landed perfectly in the middle of the ladies' tee some fifteen yards in front of me.

Hearing no laughter, I quickly glanced around to see if anyone was watching. No one. Great. I teed up another ball.

As beads of sweat formed across my brow, I shot my mulligan. The second shot also soared majestically into the bright blue Texas sky but, this time, landed about 200 yards up in the middle of the fairway. It was quite possibly the best single golf shot I'd ever made.

More importantly, no one had seen my initial gaffe, and no disaster had occurred. Two affluent-looking golfers were approaching the tee and had witnessed the second drive.

"Nice shot," one of them remarked. "Right down the middle. Hope I hit one like it."

Ever gracious in victory, I thanked him for the compliment. I wished them both a good round and prepared to leave the tee.

"Hey," the other golfer called to me. "That your ball up there on the ladies' tee?"

"No," I replied, thinking quickly. "It was there when I got here. Guess someone forgot it."

My luck held for the rest of the day. I shot under a hundred which, for me, is like winning the Masters. I didn't hurt anyone with a stray golf ball, I never ran afoul of the famous singer's bodyguards, and I didn't humiliate myself - at least not in public.

After the round, I was changing clothes in the locker room when I remembered my bargain with God. I walked back into the pro shop and pulled the attendant aside.

"Where's the nearest church?" I asked.

"Church? What kind?"

"Doesn't matter, as long as it's close."

"You mean you're looking for any kind of church and you're in a hurry to find it?" the attendant asked in disbelief.

"That's right," I explained. "When you make a golf bet with God, you don't postpone paying off."

Amen.

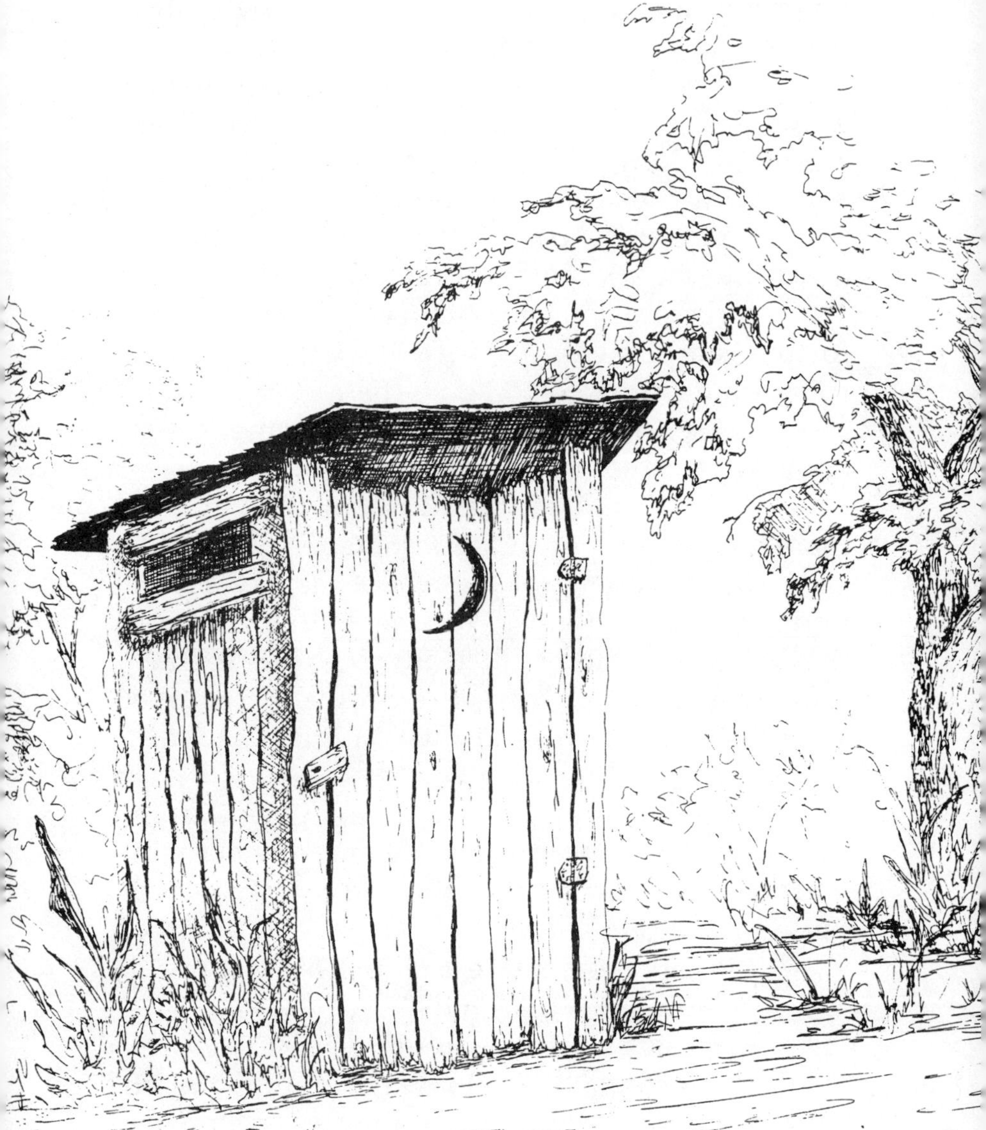

SAVE THE OUTHOUSE!

"When a man reproached him for going into unclean places, he said, 'The sun too penetrates into privies, but is not polluted by them."
                                           Diogenes

Some time back I wrote about a piece of vanishing Americana - the outhouse.

Jokingly, I suggested that we begin an effort to save the outhouse before it becomes extinct. Surprisingly, I received a tremendous amount of feedback from people offering to join the effort.

Bowing to popular demand, I am officially establishing STOP - Save Texas' Outdoor Privies - to protect these endangered monuments to our heritage. Disciples of STOP must recognize that our campaign will be a difficult one because so many people will not understand our cause. Privies are considered by some to be crude, dirty, and - well - primitive. Our first effort must be to reform and educate these poor, misguided people.

These people must learn that back before the days of individual bedrooms, "private time", and allowing someone their "personal space", outhouses were often a retreat for poor souls seeking a place of solitude for a few moments of deep contemplation. Accordingly, a well-groomed outhouse was often a source of pride for a homeowner. Privies were often painted or whitewashed, decorated, and landscaped. In Kendall County, you can still see examples of an outhouse with a trellis for climbing vines, as well as one with birdhouses built on top.

Outhouses have even been immortalized in the contemporary literature of our society. The famous poem "The Passing of the Outhouse" by James Whitcomb Riley mournfully laments the loss of the little house out back. A book, *Texas Out Back*, by Harry Anthony DeYoung, contains sketches of Texas outhouses drawn by the author in the 1920's and 1930's. Despite Mr. DeYoung's noble purpose, more than a few people were reduced to fits of laughter when approached for permission to draw their privy. Even then, some people just didn't appreciate the majesty of these noble retreats.

Now, before the last outhouse passes into history, it is time for STOP to mobilize and save these structures. Every county in the Hill Country could organize a local STOP committee. It's mission would be to preserve all remaining privies in the area. Through our local STOP Committees, we could lobby the State Historical Commission to erect markers and medallions at historically-significant outhouses. We could erect a monument on the courthouse lawn to commemorate the role of the outhouse in the settling of the Hill Country.

Think about it - a monument to the outhouse! Bizarre? Crude? Unheard of? Hardly!

In Texas, we have courthouse monuments for a mule (in Muleshoe), a pecan (in Seguin), Popeye (in Crystal City), a giant roadrunner (in Ft. Stockton), and Alley Oop (in Iraan), just to name a few. Why not a fitting monument to the outhouse?

How about a festival? We have the Oatmeal Festival in Oatmeal (where else?), Cow Patty Bingo in Slaton, the Great Texas Flea Bite Festival in Wichita Falls, and the Mountain Oyster Festival in El Paso. Surely there is a town out there somewhere that would be willing to forfeit obscurity to host the "Privy Days Festival."

Use your imagination. We could have parades and a carnival. We could have an Outhouse Queen sitting on a special throne (I'll let you use your imagination there).

We could sell commemorative caps and tee-shirts. We could have games - the Privy Olympics - such as the "How Many People Can You Get Into an Outhouse?" competition, a toilet paper throwing contest, and a 100-yard dash while holding your overalls up with one hand.

Now is the time for action, STOP members. Get organized and call your chamber of commerce today. Get involved and save the privy!

*****

TANK FISHING

As a youngster, summer was a magic time in the Texas Hill Country. It was a time to explore the fields and pastures. It was a time to ride horseback through the cedar-covered hills. It was a time to swim in the cool, clear waters of a spring-fed river. When it was time to relax, it was a time to go tank fishing.

I can't help becoming a little amused when I see people heading out to the lakes in a fishing rig that would put the Starship Enterprise to shame. Don't get me wrong; there's nothing wrong with bass boats that skim across the water at warp speed and have depth-finders and sonar equipment to help outwit the fish. It just seems like all of that takes an awful lot of effort for something I always considered a relaxing pastime.

Fishing, to me, will always mean a cane pole, worm or cricket on the line, dropped into a stock tank. That's how I spent many a summer's afternoon. Granted, I never landed anything that you would want to stuff and hang on your living room wall, but that wasn't the point. I was more interested in seeing the catch mounted in a frying pan than over the mantle.

Actually, I always considered a catfish to be the best catch simply because it was the best eating. It's just that catfishing can be a slow and uneventful process. Catching an occasional crappie or small bass on a cane pole passed the time while waiting for a hungry catfish to find the baited throwline.

My grandfather and I would have our best fishing expeditions at a stock tank on my uncle's ranch. Arriving in mid-morning, we would drop several throwlines with catfish bait beneath the pecan trees that lined the side of the tank. Getting these lines out was the important part; it was catfish we were really after.

This accomplished, we would drop our cane poles into the tank and wait for something to happen. Sometimes it did; sometimes it didn't. Sometimes we would catch a few fish; often we would just eat peanut butter sandwiches before dozing off for a nap.

At the end of the day came the highlight of the fishing trip - checking the lines for catfish. If we had been lucky, we had a couple of good ones that Oma would fry up for supper. If not, we'd have a great excuse to go fishing again.

When I think of fishing, the images that come to mind are sitting on the bank of the stock tank, watching the cork bob in the water; lying back on the soft, moist ground watching the clouds go by; the warm summer breeze blowing through the pecan trees. No outboard motors, no reels, no "can't miss" lures - just a quiet afternoon with a cane pole, a can of worms, and the knowledge that, if the fish didn't bite, you could come back again ... soon.

*****

UNLUCKY LINDY

Three years before his famous flight to Paris, Charles Lindbergh became a part of Hill Country lore when he crashed into a store at Camp Wood in Real County. Not-so-lucky Lindy and his barnstorming partner, Leon Klink, were flying through Texas before reporting for Army Air Corps training when an attempted take-off from a main street in Camp Wood sent the Lone Eagle's plane into the wall of the Puett Hardware Store.

It was January of 1924, and Lindbergh and Klink were barnstorming while enroute to training at Brooks Field in San Antonio. With time to spare before induction, the pioneer aviators decided to fly west from the Alamo City. Spotting the West Nueces River, the duo thought they had reached the Rio Grande and flew up river until they arrived at the community of Camp Wood.

The flyers landed and taxied Lindbergh's surplus Curtiss Jenny to the town square. Once they had gotten their bearings, they decided to stay the night and attend a dance before taking off again in the morning.

The next day, Lindbergh surveyed the area for a departure route. Only one street was wide enough for take-off; but just barely. The plane would have to pass between two telephone poles that were 46 feet apart. The wing span of the Jenny was 44 feet - two feet to spare.

The engine roared. The crowd was curious. Lindbergh was confident. Such a take-off was only mildly challenging for a seasoned barnstormer and, besides, measurements had shown that the two-foot margin was plenty to ensure a successful ascent. Everything had been considered. Everything, that is, except for a hole in the road.

As the plane lurched forward, bearing down on the critical area between the two poles, the landing gear hit the previously-unnoticed pot hole. The Jenny veered to the side, the right wing hit one of the poles, causing the plane to swerve out of control.

The nose of the plane crashed into the wall of the hardware store, scattering merchandise and pieces of airplane across the street. Although he sustained only a bruised ego, Lindy's moniker of "Lucky" would not be earned in Real County, Texas.

The merchant refused to accept any money for the damages, apparently recognizing the tremendous promotional value of owning the only hardware store in the Hill Country to survive a plane crash. For months afterward, people came to see the building that had been hit by an airplane and the merchant's business prospered.

The plane, although damaged, was repaired within several days. The battered Curtiss Jenny once again airworthy, Lindbergh and Klink were on their way back to San Antonio, leaving the Puett Hardware Store as a footnote in history and a Hill Country legend.

*****

PORCH SITTIN' TALK

Opa and I were sitting on the porch the other night, just talking about things in general. Opa, you see, is an expert on things in general. He is, to put it mildly, opinionated and he's glad to share his opinions with anyone who'll listen.

"You still livin' in that condom?" he asked.

"It's condominium, Opa. Yes, I still live in a condominium," I replied.

"Humph. You just end up sharing other people's roaches in one of those things. It got one of them hot tubs in it?"

"Well, a jacuzzi, yes. Why?" I asked as if I didn't know what was coming.

"You just be careful about who you let in that thing. People got all kinds of diseases nowadays."

The conversation went on like that for awhile as Opa provided insightful commentary on my lifestyle. He noted that I should not drive a red car ("Only lawyers and women of ill repute drive red cars"), and that I wear a suit and tie and work in an office ("If you learn a skill working with your hands, you'll always find work. Besides, sitting at a desk is bad for your heart.")

"You playing golf nowadays, huh?"

I knew that one was coming.

"Silly game; a waste of time. All you do is hit a stupid little ball and then chase after it. When you find it, you hit it again. What kind of game is that? Baseball, now there's a sport. At least in baseball, someone else has to get the ball when you hit it."

I used to get the feeling from these talks that Opa was disappointed in me. Now I've come to realize that this is just his way of passing the values of his generation on to mine. It's also his way of saying that he's concerned about me.

Opa worked with his hands all his life. He worked hard to provide for his family. Weekends only meant that he didn't start work until later in the day.

Money was meant to be saved, not squandered on foolishness. A vacation meant a couple of days visiting relatives in a nearby town. Eating out, which was rare, meant going to a catfish restaurant near Sattler, and not spending over ten dollars.

He's never flown in an airplane; he's never lived farther than 30 miles from where he was born; he's never aspired to greatness as most people define it. He wore a tuxedo only once in his life - as best man in my wedding. In many ways, I envy all of that.

He's lived a life that has been fulfilling. His family did not have what most would consider wealth, but they never wanted for food, shelter, and love.

When someone needed help, he has always been there to offer what he could. He may not have had much, but whatever he had was offered without question.

I envy all of that as well.

Someday, I would like to have earned the

right to sit on the front porch and provide the same commentary for my grandchildren; to have earned the right to be just a bit irascible, just a bit contrary.

Opa earned that right.

*****

RIDING IN THE BED OF A PICKUP TRUCK

"Have you ever ridden in the bed of a pickup truck?" I asked my wife one day.

"Of course not!" she sniffed indignantly.

She looked at me as though I just asked her if she had ever wrestled professionally or won a tobacco-spitting contest. I knew that look. It was a look that said "proper people never ride in the bed of a pickup truck".

My wife was raised as a "proper" Baptist. She was taught that one did not drink, smoke, dance, shoot pool, date Italians who live over grocery stores, and about a hundred other things that might possibly make life more enjoyable. Riding in the bed of a pickup truck was apparently somewhere on that list.

Admittedly, riding in the bed of a pickup truck is a little bit like passing gas in public - it's difficult to do while retaining one's personal dignity. However, there are those who seem right at home in a truck bed, and even those who relish such an opportunity.

There are certain times, places, and people

that are right at home in a truck bed. Farm kids riding in a truck piled full of hay seem to enjoy riding high atop the haystacks. In fact, farm kids typically seem right at home in the back of a pickup truck.

Construction workers and oilfield hands often ride in the back of a truck. This is partly out of necessity since both pickups and a large crew of workers are required at job sites. When it's time to go somewhere, there's just not enough room in the front of the truck.

Beachgoers often ride in the bed of a pickup truck. When you arrive at a crowded beach, you just drop the tailgate and you have an instant sun deck. Some even set up outdoor lounge chairs, lather up with suntan oil, and start working on their tan from the back of the truck while on the way to the beach.

There are those who seem embarrassed about the whole thing and sit real low so only the top of their heads stick out. Others, however, sit up high so they can smile and wave at everyone they pass. You can usually tell these folks after a long journey - they're the ones with their hair sticking straight back and bugs in their teeth.

There are times and places, though, where truck-bed-riding is completely inappropriate. For example, you should never arrive at a wedding (especially your own), or any formal event, in the back of a truck.

You should never arrive at a Baptist church in the bed of a pickup. If you do, they'll talk about you during the sermon - from the pulpit.

It is equally gauche to ride in the back of a pickup while in a funeral procession. Out of respect to the dearly-departed, everyone should crowd into the cab and hope that all remembered to use enough deodorant.

Likewise, the dearly-departed should never have to ride to his or her reward in the back of a pickup. It just doesn't look right, and all the flowers will blow off.

You never want to ride in a pickup bed in places where rich folks live in expensive homes. The Highland Park area of Dallas, the Woodlands in Houston, Alamo Heights in San Antonio, or any area community built around a golf course will probably call the cops on you if you're seen riding in the bed of a pickup.

So what kind of people ride in the back of pickup trucks? Here are some general guidelines:

George Bush has probably ridden in the back of a pickup, but wouldn't admit it - Barbara Bush probably has, and enjoyed it.

Nancy Reagan would never ride in a truck bed - Ronald Reagan probably has, but can't remember for certain.

Willie Nelson and Jerry Jeff Walker would be the kind to smile and wave while riding in the back of a truck - George Strait wouldn't because he'd lose his $400 cowboy hat and dirty his dry-cleaned blue jeans.

Donald Trump never has, but might have to get used to it if he keeps throwing all his money away on every expensive bimbo he runs into.

Burt Reynolds would - Meryl Streep wouldn't. Both should be self-explanatory.

Zsa Zsa Gabor would never consider it, which is probably fortunate for us all. The sight of Zsa Zsa with wind-blown makeup and no wig would probably scare everyone else off the road.

How about our own Texas politicians? Which of them would ride in the back of a pickup truck?

Speaker of the House Gib Lewis? Probably not. He shows about 173 teeth when he smiles, and it would take weeks to clean them all after a ride.

Attorney General "Dandy" Dan Morales? Are you kidding? He'd wrinkle his suit and muss his hair. Besides, he'd never do anything unless he saw Henry Cisneros do it first.

Agriculture Commissioner Rick Perry has probably ridden in the back of a pickup truck more times than he can remember. Former Ag-Commissioner Jim Hightower couldn't tell the difference between a pickup truck and a snow-blower.

Governor Ann Richards? I don't think it would be possible. Just imagine what that 3-foot-tall bouffant hairdo would look like after the ride. She'd have to call out the National Guard just to pile it all back on top of her head.

How about her arch-rival, that silver-tongued former gubernatorial candidate Clayton Williams? Absolutely. In fact, he'd probably prefer to ride during a rainstorm so he could "just lay back and enjoy it".

And that might just be the best philosophy to have about riding in the back of a pickup truck. As Clayton would advise, "If it's inevitable, just lay back and enjoy it."

*****

DIE SCHEUTZENVEREIN

It's just before dawn. The first light of day is barely visible on the horizon. The dew is fresh and the sweet smell of cedar hangs heavily in the moist morning air. In the distance, you can hear the sound of approaching vehicles, faintly at first, but growing louder as a small caravan of trucks winds its way up the narrow dirt trail.

The trucks lumber to a halt and voices emerge from the still of the morning. Excited voices, speaking in German, are punctuated by the sound of rifle bolts being opened and closed.

The weapons are carefully checked and inspected by the marksmen. They cannot afford a missed shot; a wasted bullet could mean failure. They all know the odds - on this day, only one of them would emerge victorious.

Sound like the beginning of a war movie? You're close. This is dawn at a scheutzenverein - a traditional German shooting club. The shooters will all be seeking the same elusive prize - the title of king of the marksmen.

There are still many scheutzenverein hidden away in the hills and cedar breaks of the Hill Country and, as has always been the custom, they are the sites of some of the most fierce gun battles this side of Beirut. All shooters arrive in hopes of becoming the Scheutzenkoenig -the "shooting king" - for a year.

A scheutzenverein was typically the first

social club organized by German settlers upon their arrival in the Hill Country. In fact, the New Braunfels Scheutzenverein claims the title of the oldest continuously-operating shooting club in the United States, having been founded on July 4, 1845, just three months after the founding of the town.

The settlers believed in playing as hard as they worked, and the "social" rifle competition was intense. Even more fierce was the competition between neighboring clubs. Most clubs even designed club flags to be flown at all competitions, a practice which continues to this day.

Despite the furious competition, a day at the scheutzenverein was a family affair. The serious shooters - which was just about every man who could lift and aim a rifle - often arrived at dawn to clean their weapons, check their windage, and get in a little practice.

The families usually arrived later in the morning, bringing along a large picnic lunch. Initially, ladies were not allowed to participate; however, most clubs later permitted the wives and sisters of members to become "associate" members, competing among themselves in special target events.

The competition usually lasted throughout the afternoon until one club won a decisive victory, or until the "king" was crowned. The day's shooting done, the guns would be carefully cleaned and stored as the the evening's barbecue was being prepared. Music and dancing lasted well into the night.

So serious were these competitions, that

many continued during war years despite a shortage of ammunition. Throughout these difficult times, every shooter was allowed one - and only one - shot to determine who would reign as the top marksman for the next year.

So as the morning still is broken by the arrival of the steely-eyed marksmen, the whitetail deer need not run. The whitewing doves need not fly. Even the lowly raccoons need not fear. They are not today's target.

For members of the Scheutzenverein, the only trophy that counts is a silver loving-cup and the title of "King of the Marksmen."

*****

EMMA'S NEW OUTHOUSE

Emma and Otto Schwartz were typical Hill Country folks. Certainly not wealthy, but they managed a good living raising a few goats and pigs, selling eggs, and farming a small plot of bottom land near the Guadalupe River between Comfort and Center Point.

While Otto worked the farm, Emma cooked, cleaned, and kept their tidy little home. In fact, Emma, a large woman, particularly enjoyed baking cookies, cakes, and pies. Her German-chocolate cake was legendary at the pot-luck dinners down at the Lutheran church, and the only thing Emma enjoyed more than baking was eating the finished product.

Emma's love for pastry, quite naturally, only contributed to her ample size. This never seemed a problem for her, or Otto, until Emma outgrew the outhouse.

Tired of having to squeeze in and out of the privy, Emma begged Otto to provide a larger facility.

"Please, Otto. It's just too little. I'm having trouble getting the door to close," she pleaded.

"Ach, you're getting soft, woman! If the door won't close, just leave it open," said Otto, dismissing the request. "Who's going to see, the pigs?"

"And what if the ladies from the church come to visit," Emma shot back, "and see me sitting there with the door open. What will they say?"

Otto was unimpressed. He'd always considered the church ladies as busy-bodies who only visited to gossip and make sure that Emma would continue to bring German-chocolate cakes to the church dinners.

"Well, what if Pastor Schmidt comes to visit?" Emma insisted. "What would he think?"

Actually, Otto didn't much care what Pastor Schmidt thought. The only time the preacher "visited" was just before supper when he knew he'd be invited to stay for the meal. However, Pastor Schmidt was one of those preachers who named names during church, and Otto had no desire to be the subject of some future sermon on the sin of not providing your wife with proper bathroom facilities.

Otto relented. Construction would begin the next day.

Dawn was greeted with the sound of a pick-axe breaking ground. By noon, Otto had excavated a pit big enough to be a root cellar. By mid-afternoon, the frame of a new, spacious privy was taking shape. If he had to go to this much trouble, Otto was going to make this comfort station a showplace.

Once the outside of the project was completed, Otto decided to customize the interior to further accommodate his wife's ample needs by hand-carving an oversized hole. A little larger target could only add to Emma's comfort, Otto theorized.

Within a week, the job was finished. The new outhouse was a sight to behold. Not only was it extra large with a custom-designed seating area, it had a fine wooden-plank floor and a shiny tin roof. A thing of beauty and, hopefully, a joy forever for the now-smiling Emma.

The next morning, Otto was rewarded with a breakfast of eggs, bacon, hotcakes, and blueberry muffins. Emma was still smiling. All was right with the world as Otto headed out to tend his neglected corn field.

With Otto gone, Emma decided it was time to try out the unspoiled privy. Armed with the newest Sears-Roebuck catalog, she settled comfortably in, intending to take full advantage of the spacious new facility that her loving husband had built for her.

Emma was so happy, she probably didn't even hear scratching sounds coming from beneath her. Even if she heard the noises from below, she probably thought that the building was just settling. But when the distinctive odor hit her, particularly from a brand-new outhouse, Emma knew that something was dreadfully wrong.

At that moment, she felt the sensation of something cold and wet nudging urgently against her expansive posterior. Screaming with horror, Emma came up off the seat like a NASA rocket.

As quickly as the seat was vacated, an extremely agitated skunk struggled to escape from the pit below. It seems that Emma had unknowingly sealed the only entrance to what the skunk had thought was going to be it's new den.

Fortunately, both parties escaped suffering only mental anguish. The skunk never returned to the privy. Neither did Emma. Poor Otto, faced with his wife's adamant refusal to ever again set foot (or anything else) in the outhouse, dismantled his masterpiece and used the wood to build a new chicken coop.

And Emma? Well, she had seen one of those new-fangled indoor toilets in town...

*****

MY FATHER THE BULLFIGHTER

From the time he saw his first rodeo at the age of four, my father, Weldon, wanted to ride bulls. As soon as he was old enough, he would practice by riding horses...or mules ...or goats...or anything else that would hold still. He couldn't wait to grow up and join the rodeo.

As a teenager, Dad had two great interests: girls and bullriding. Since he had better luck with the bulls than with the girls, he started rodeoing as soon as he was out of high school.

Rodeoing has always been a tough sport.

You pay your own way to the rodeo; you buy your own equipment; you pay your own entry fees; and, most importantly, you pay your own medical bills. The only way you come out ahead is if you win the purse for your event. Forty years ago, even if you won, those purses weren't much to brag about.

It certainly wasn't glamorous. The bulls won more often than my father did, leaving him in the dust with a bruised ego and no payday. Occasionally he would wake up in the bed of a battered pickup truck being driven to some small-town hospital.

Dad will proudly show you the trophy buckles he won during his rodeo career. One year, he was the number-one bullrider in the nation, and was third in the all-around cowboy competition.

He can also show you scars the bulls and broncs left on him. He can show you where the doctors reconstructed a knee; where they put a plate in his arm; and where his hip was put back together with a surgical pin. When he flies, he drives the security people at the airport crazy. With all of the metal holding his body together, he'd set off a metal detector even if he tried to walk through naked.

Despite all the hardships, my father still loved the rodeo and tried to pass his appreciation of the sport on to me. I, however, never warmed up to being pitched face first into the dirt off the back of angry livestock, especially with several hundred people watching.

I guess Dad loved to rodeo so much

because he loved to ride anything that presented a challenge. Bullriding was his favorite, but he also tried his hand at bareback bronc riding and saddle bronc riding.

One time, while rodeoing in southern Arizona, my father met up with a Mexican cowboy named Luis Martinez. The two struck up a quick friendship and Luis invited Dad to a bullfight across the border in Nogales, Mexico.

After watching the first bullfight, my father was confused.

"Luis," he asked his host, "isn't anyone gonna try to ride that bull?"

Luis patiently explained that riding the bull was not a part of the sport of bullfighting.

"Seems like a waste of a perfectly good bull," my father observed, "Why, I'll bet you case of beer that I could ride that critter."

"Señor Weldon," his host patiently explained, "these bulls are much too dangerous to ride."

That was as close to a challenge as my father needed.

The arena crowd watched in amazement as the loco gringo jumped into the bullring and crept up behind the bull. An equally-astonished matador wisely began to back away from the entire proceedings.

As the bull watched the matador retreat, Dad jumped onto the confused animal's back, wrapped an arm around each horn, laid flat, and held on for the ride of his life.

For a moment, the bewildered beast just stood there. Then it did the only natural thing -

it ran for its life. The terrified bull made three complete circles of the bullring with the insane cowboy on its back. On the third lap, Dad was pitched off into the dirt.

The bull continued to run until someone opened a gate and allowed the poor creature to escape into a tunnel beneath the stands. It was reported that the animal broke through the barrier at the other end of the tunnel and was last seen running toward Tijuana with a terrified look in its eyes.

Luis made his way to my father's side as the crowd cheered and chanted wildly.

"I guess I owe you some beer, compadre," Luis laughed as he helped Dad to his feet.

"You sure do," my father said as the crowd continued to shout. "Say, what's all the chanting about?"

"Like all great matadors, the crowd has given you a name," Luis explained. "You should acknowledge them; it's the custom."

Ever gracious in victory, Weldon the bullfighter dusted himself off and waved and bowed as the crowd continued to chant:

"Viva! Viva! Viva, el Stupido!"

*****

"GOD BLESS YOU, FOR SPOTTY AND ME"

Not long ago, I was walking with a friend in downtown San Antonio. As we strolled along Houston Street near Alamo Plaza, I was reminded of the days when I would stop and visit with Blind Herman as he sat at a downtown corner, waiting for someone to drop a couple of coins into his cup.

"What ever happened to Blind Herman?" I asked my companion.

"Blind Herman. That's someone I haven't thought of in years," came the reply. "I don't really know; I guess he must be dead now."

Herman Bednorz was a fixture on those downtown streets for years. Herman had lost his sight in an explosion at a construction site in the 1940's. After that, he was forced to scratch out a bare living by asking for "donations" on the street. No one ever referred to Herman as a beggar.

Literally hundreds of people a day walked right past him and his faithful dog, Spotty. Many were too busy to bother with a blind man and a mutt dog. Others looked down upon the pair with disdain. Some cast occasional glances at the man with his tin cup; most didn't really care.

"A little spare change for Spotty and Me?" was the question he would repeatedly ask to no one in particular as the crowds rushed by. Herman always included Spotty in his request.

"Spotty ain't one of them trained seeing-eye dogs," Herman once told me. "He's just a mutt that wandered up one day and hung around. I fed him a part of my sandwich and he's been with me ever since. I guess we get along so good because we're both pretty pitiful."

Just as Herman took care of Spotty, the devoted pooch watched over his blind master. The dog would carefully eye the people walking by, especially those that walked up to put something in the cup. If you lingered, Spotty would quietly stand and watch. As soon as you spoke to

Herman and received a response, the dog would relax.

Those passers-by who cared enough to drop some spare change in the cup were always politely thanked. If you put some folding money into the cup, it was always a "God bless you, for Spotty and me."

There were also those who would stop for a minute to chat with Herman while dropping some money in the cup. The downtown beat cops, whose job included keeping panhandlers off the street, were always good for a dollar or two. The true angels, however, were the clerks, secretaries, and storekeepers who would religiously check on Herman and Spotty.

These few loyal friends would always make sure that Herman had shade and Spotty had fresh water during the hot summer months. In the cold of the winter, they made sure that Herman and Spotty had a warm coat and blankets.

On those particularly bitter-cold days, the manager of one downtown five-and-dime store would always invite Herman and his dog inside for shelter. The routine was always the same: Herman would, at first, refuse the offer, telling the manager that "a blind man and a dog just ain't good for your business". The store manager would insist that he and Spotty at least come in "just long enough to warm up", and have a hot cup of coffee.

The "just long enough to warm up" usually ended up being all day. Just when Herman was about to head back outside, one of the waitresses would refill Herman's coffee or give him a sandwich, explaining that "the cook made one too many".

Spotty, too, would get his share of "scraps" from the kitchen. More often than not, the "scraps" were specially prepared for the old dog.

When closing time rolled around, Herman would always find a ten-dollar bill in his cup. "One of the customers must have put it in there" was always the explanation the manager gave him.

I last saw Herman and Spotty in the summer of 1970, sitting in their usual spot. The heat was oppressive, and someone had constructed a makeshift shelter on the street corner to protect the pair.

"Hello, Herman," I said. "How are you and Spotty getting along in this heat?"

"Oh, pretty good, I guess," the blind man replied, "but it's sure hot. Spotty here's getting old and the heat's pretty hard on him. The beat cops told me to go ahead and move down to the river walk where there's shade and water."

"Anything I can get for you?" I asked.

"No, but we appreciate the offer. That's one of the great things about these people downtown," Herman observed. "They care enough about a run-down blind man and an old mongrel dog to help us out when we need it. They really care about us. I only wish I could see their faces."

I dropped some money in his cup and wished the blind man luck.

"God bless you," he said, "for Spotty and me."

*****

AUTUMN IN THE HILL COUNTRY

*****

THE INFAMOUS CHICKEN-SUIT CAPER

Driving down the street the other day, I passed a new fried chicken restaurant. There was a person standing out front wearing a chicken suit, waving to passing motorists and trying to attract customers. Wearing a chicken suit is sort of like riding in the back of a pickup truck - there's no way to do either with dignity. I know of both from personal experience.

As a third-grader at Mirabeau B. Lamar Elementary School, I was selected to be in the annual school play. Since very few third-graders were ever picked for the play, I was extremely proud of myself. Proud, that is, until I found out that I was supposed play the part of a barnyard chicken.

Not just any chicken, mind you, but an Ancona chicken. For those of you who may not be intimately familiar with the various chicken breeds, the Ancona is a breed which originated in Italy. They are predominantly dark in color with white speckles on the back feathers and saddle.

I felt bad enough that I had to play a

chicken, but a spotted immigrant chicken was almost more humiliation than I could bear. I was then informed that my contribution to this theatrical event would be to dance around like I was scratching in the dirt while the older kids - playing farmers - sang a song about chickens.

The play's perennial director was a somewhat-effeminate fifth-grade teacher named Sidney Blumentritt. Sidney was described by town folks as being "blessed with an overabundance of artistic flair". He took his job directing the school play seriously, and insisted that my Ancona chicken costume be as accurate as possible.

Sidney sent home a sketch of what he thought my costume should look like. Oma took one look at the sketch and, wanting to make sure I was the best chicken to ever strut across the school stage, set out to create the finest chicken suit this side of Hollywood. She even met with Sidney on several occasions to make sure the tail feathers met with his approval.

Finally, the big night arrived. Since the school had no dressing rooms, I had to get dressed at home. The suit consisted of a round body of black fabric over a wire frame, tail feathers made from more fabric wrapped over wire, yellow knee-length stockings, and yellow chicken feet covering my sneakers.

The crowning piece de resistance was a full head, complete with a yellow beak and red comb and wattles. Oma was so proud of the chicken suit that she insisted I show Opa our handiwork before we left for school. As I emerged from the bedroom in all my chicken-glory, Opa glanced up from the newspaper, took one look at me, dropped his cigar, and laughed so hard that he looked like he was having convulsions. He was still laughing hysterically when Oma ushered me out the door.

Not yet convinced that my confidence had been sufficiently bolstered, Oma took me next door to show the costume to Mrs. Silver. Once she recovered from the shock of finding a three-foot-tall chicken knocking on her door, Mrs. Silver was extremely gracious.

"My, what a lovely buzzard you make," she said with a smile.

"He's not a buzzard, Louella," Oma quickly corrected. "He's a chicken. An Ancona chicken. They're from Italy."

"Oh, of course," our neighbor apologized, "Without my glasses on, I can't tell an Italian chicken from a buzzard."

A common mistake, no doubt.

Since it was impossible to ride in the cab of our pickup without damaging the chicken costume, Oma had me ride in the bed of the truck on the way to the school.

"Make sure you crouch down and stay close to the cab," she told me, "we don't want the wind to blow any of your feathers off."

Crouch down? I would have gladly laid flat beneath a tarp to avoid being spotted riding to school in the bed of a pickup truck dressed in a chicken suit.

Once at school, Sidney immediately ran to us, gushing about how wonderful my costume was. The kids, of course, didn't share his appreciation. Most of them were doubled up with laughter, not unlike Opa.

Backstage, the only kid that would come near me was Elroy Dietert. He was playing a goat in the third act, and his costume was almost as silly as mine.

When my time in the spotlight finally arrived, I managed to perform my little dance flawlessly, scratching for worms in the imaginary barnyard of the school stage. I didn't trip and fall. I didn't lose any part of my costume. And because of the music and singing, I didn't hear the howls of laughter when I appeared on stage.

After the play, I started to pull off the hated chicken suit as soon as we got to the truck.

"Now you be careful with that suit," Oma told me. "We don't want to get it damaged.

"What difference does it make?" I asked. "The play's over with. We can just throw it away."

"Throw it away? Of course not!" Oma said with a shocked look on her face. "We might be able to use it again."

"There'll be a different play next year, Oma. It probably won't have chickens in it at all," I said hopefully.

"Well, maybe not," she explained, "but you'll need something for Halloween."

From that day forward, I never went trick-or-treating again.

*****

ROADSIDE DINOSAURS

At one time, you could see them every few miles along the back roads of the Texas Hill Country. Today, they are an endangered species; yet another victim of an increasingly-urban lifestyle. The victim: the roadside ice house.

They were known by many names - beer joints, juke joints, roadhouses, or taverns. Regardless of the name, they were friendly roadside gathering places where folks could socialize and enjoy one another's company after a hard day's work. Oh yes, I almost forgot - this was usually done over a cold beer. Or two. Or more.

The names would usually be something like the Dew Drop Inn, Otto's Place, Shorty's Drive-Inn, or (my personal favorite) Bier Hier. The names may have differed, but they generally all looked alike - a plain little building with a collection of dusty pickup trucks parked in the gravel parking lot.

The front of the joint was often decorated faded beer signs and slogans like "Can You Get From Here to There Without a Six-Pack?" The typical farmer or rancher, spotting such a sign, would invariably come to the realization that he, in fact, could not get to "there" without refreshment.

In the summer, you could retreat from the heat of the day, catch up on the latest gossip, and quench your thirst with a cold Shiner beer. In the winter, you could warm up next to the pot-bellied stove, catch up on the latest gossip, and quench your thirst with a cold Shiner beer. In case you weren't aware, a cold Shiner beer is an appropriate thirst-quencher regardless of season - sort of a German Gatorade.

Evenings at the ice houses were family affairs. They were a gathering spot for the rural families. The old men would pull tables together and play dominoes. The old ladies would gather to talk. The younger couples could dance to Ernest Tubb and Hank Thompson on the juke box while their kids played out in the parking lot. No drunks, foul language, or fights were tolerated. This was a family place and everyone knew to respect it.

Ice houses often served other purposes as well. Some carried a few groceries and had a gas pump; some served as rural post offices; some were school bus drop-off points. These were not dark, sinful bars for the notorious element; they were friendly places where rural folks mingled.

Only a few such ice houses remain. Like roadside dinosaurs, they are quickly becoming extinct. Most have been replaced by convenience chain stores offering the same groceries and gasoline, but with everything else from video-tape rentals to "hot-to-go" foods. You can still get that cold bottle of Shiner, but you have to take it home. You may then drink it as you eat your "hot-to-go" barbecue sandwich and watch your rented movie.

If you want to go out for a social drink, there are trendy pubs with ferns hanging from the ceiling, "theme nights," and specialty drinks that involve sparkling water and a twist of some sort of imported fruit. The bartender will look at you like you've stepped in something disgusting if you order a Shiner.

The ice houses are all but gone, victims of our changing lifestyle. Maybe it's just as well. The old Dew Drop Inn just wouldn't be the same with a BMW or a Mercedes in the gravel parking lot. Junior executives, resplendent in their Italian designer suits and power ties wouldn't want to "network" over a game of dominoes.

And there's just no way to serve a Shiner with a twist.

*****

BODO RIDES AGAIN

I've mentioned my boyhood friend, Bodo Schwamkrug, before. Bodo was big, dumb, and country, but he was one of my best friends. Although Bodo was older than me, we often were in the same grade because he was occasionally "held back" in school. I'm not sure that Bodo was really dumb, he just didn't see any need for school since all he ever wanted to do in life was drive a dump truck - a red dump truck with his name on the door.

"Them teachers won't tell you how to drive a backhoe or shift a dump truck," Bodo would tell me, "and I ain't gonna need to know any of that other stuff."

People tried to explain to Bodo that he, in fact, would need all that other stuff but, being a hard-core German, he wasn't about to be persuaded by mere facts. As it turned out, Bodo was right. He later made a mint running a hauling business and driving his cherry-red dump truck.

Bodo was just as stubborn in other things. Bodo never accepted the concept of "couldn't." If you told him he couldn't do something, it was a challenge he had to accept - if for no other reason than to prove to you that he could.

In high school, Bodo drove a 1960 Chevrolet that looked like a veteran of several demolition derbies. On one occasion, Bodo decided that since his car was, as usual, up on blocks needing repair, he would just ride a horse to school.

"Bodo," I told him, "you can't ride a horse to school. It's against the rules. Besides, where would you tie it up?"

"I'll just tie it out front of the school," he said calmly, "Right under the big oak trees."

Sure enough, Bodo kept his promise. The next morning, his horse was tied beneath the oak trees right in front of the high school. It just so happened that those trees were located right next to the faculty parking lot.

It took exactly three minutes for Assistant Principal Bill "the Vulture" Long to spot the horse tied in front of the school. As luck would have it, he spotted the horse just as the animal was relieving itself right next to the principal's car. It took another five seconds for the Vulture to figure out who was responsible.

Bodo immediately received an invitation to the administration office to have a chat about his choice of transportation.

"Bodo, what is that horse doing in front of the school?" asked the exasperated assistant principal.

"Probably just standing there, but I can run outside and check for you," Bodo responded. Bodo had figured he was in trouble and wanted to appear as cooperative as possible.

"Don't be a smart-aleck, boy," the Vulture shot back, "we've put up with an awful lot from you. I remember last semester when you glued the nude girlie pin-ups inside the required-reading books in the library. I thought that poor librarian was going to have a stroke when she found them."

Bodo stared at the floor to hide the smirk on his face. That one was one of his favorite practical jokes.

"And do you might remember the time you took the transmission out of the band bus?"

"I was only borrowing it to put in my car for the weekend, Mr. Long," Bodo pleaded. "I would have put it back..."

"I don't want to hear it," the Vulture cut him off. "You seem to have an absolute disregard for the rules of this school. But this horse matter, this really tops the list. I have a good mind to suspend you from school for a couple of days."

"Suspend me?" Bodo asked. "You mean I can't come to school?"

That was like offering an alcoholic a drink.

"Tell you what, Mr. Long," Bodo suggested, "make it a week and you've got a deal."

The Vulture turned a deep shade of scarlet. Obviously the impact of a suspension would be lost on this particular miscreant. Instead, it was decided that Bodo would have to attend an extra study hall for the remainder of the semester.

"Well, Bodo," I asked him afterward, "did you learn anything from all of this?"

"I sure did," he nodded emphatically, "them faculty people don't like anyone even parking near their lot. The next time I'm going to have to tie my horse out back - in the student parking lot."

*****

KATZENMUSIK

A couple of friends of mine recently got married. The service was moving; the bride was beautiful; the mother was crying; the groom was terrified. In short, the perfect wedding.

The evening was capped by a first-class reception at a country club with a full meal for all guests, several huge cakes, plenty of drinks, and a 15-piece mariachi band. As much fun as we all had, I couldn't help but think about how much more fun it would have been if there would have been a shivaree.

For those of you who have never been a

part of a shivaree - sometimes spelled chivaree - you've missed out on one of the top ten customs in the world. Basically, a shivaree is when the wedding guests permit the newlyweds to escape from the wedding and reception, but then follow them home to surprise them on their wedding night. Sound like fun? Sound like a good way to get shot? Right on both counts.

In German, a shivaree is called katzenmusik. Literally translated this means "cat music," which is probably as accurate a term as you can come up with. The traditional German katzenmusik, as was once widely practiced throughout the Hill Country, involved the men arriving at the newlywed's home first. They announced their arrival by shouting, dragging tin cans, beating on washtubs, ringing cowbells, and firing shotguns into the air.

After the men had gotten the attention of the bride and groom, the women would bring along some food and small gifts, presumably to apologize for the rude intrusion the newlyweds had just suffered. In case I didn't mention it before, the consumption of large quantities of beer typically accompanied these festivities.

Once confronted by this mob, the newlyweds were socially obligated to play host for the rest of the evening. Dancing, drinking, and general celebrating typically continued until daybreak.

The last shivaree that I attended was in rural Comal County about 20 years ago. Unfortunately, the marriage being celebrated only lasted about six months. Judging from the way the party was going when I left, that was about the time the last party-goer finally went home.

As the Hill Country has changed from rural to suburban, shivarees have become virtually extinct. Today, a gang of semi-inebriates showing up at the home of a couple of newlyweds, hollering, noise-making, shooting, and drinking would most probably be considered socially unacceptable by the neighbors.

And what a shame that is - some people just have no appreciation for tradition.

*****

VOTE FOR BONEHEAD

Run for the hills! Protect your children! Most importantly, cover your wallets - the Texas Legislature is threatening to go back into session.

In case you've been in a blissful coma, the Legislature has been in almost continuous session for what seems an eternity, thanks to an endless string of special sessions. Last year, our silly solons came up with a new school financing plan that was meant to "equalize" school funding throughout the state.

English-language translation: everyone has to pay higher taxes.

More recently, the task was to adopt and fund a state budget. Our politicians were quick to reassure us that they had their collective finger on the pulse of Texas, and recognized the "will of the people" not to raise taxes.

They talked about austerity. Massive cuts in the state bureaucracy were proposed. State Comptroller John Sharp presented a comprehensive plan to reduce waste. Chants of "no new taxes" could be heard from every nook and cranny of the capitol.

Thirty days and a dome-full of hot air later, our elected egomaniacs passed a record $59.4 billion-dollar budget. They also passed a bill providing for $2.63 billion dollars in "revenue enhancement" to fund the budget.

English-language translation: everyone has to pay higher taxes.

Texans have always recognized how dangerous legislators can be. That's why we only let them meet in regular session once every two years. Unfortunately, we forgot to limit the number of special sessions they could have. That little oversight is what's come back to haunt us.

The oldest political joke in Texas - Henry B. Gonzales doesn't count - asks what is the most dangerous time to be in Texas. Answer: When the Texas Legislature is in session.

To be fair, however, we must recognize that we voters must share in the blame for this situation. Texans have never taken their politicians seriously.

For many years, several rural Hill Country counties were represented by a little-known legislator named Benno "Bonehead" Zunker. Bonehead held office for years simply because his constituents felt he was a "safe" choice.

"Bonehead may not be much," my father used to say, "but he's got my vote because he's too dumb to steal."

Uncle Emil Dischinger was Benno's best friend since boyhood. Because of their long friendship, Uncle Emil became Benno's campaign manager during election years. Emil's campaign technique suited the talents of his uniquely-untalented candidate.

"Benno's basically harmless," Emil would reassure the voters down at the ice house. "Besides, what would he do if he didn't get re-elected? He'd end up back home on relief."

There was little the rural Hill Country folks could feel superior to, so the idea that virtually everyone was smarter than their state representative made the constitutents a little more comfortable. Within his district, "Too Dumb to Steal" quickly became Bonehead's unofficial campaign slogan.

Bonehead's terms were, not surprisingly, uneventful. He did his best to stay away from anything even remotely controversial, and voted along with the other representatives from the Hill Country. The only thing he ever introduced on the floor of the House of Representatives was a resolution commending the local football team for a winning season.

Consequently, Benno was honored for this legislative effort during a ceremony at his old high school. As a token of appreciation for not doing anything stupid while in Austin, Benno was presented with a framed football jersey emblazoned with his name and the number 60 on the back.

After the ceremony, the high school principal was asked if the jersey number was the same as the one Benno wore playing football for his alma mater.

"Heck, Benno never played football," the principal explained, "He was too lazy. We picked the number 60 because that's the highest grade he ever made."

Benno continued to be re-elected year after year. The key to Benno's successful re-election was that the people were reassured that he hadn't yet done anything stupid. Folks figured Bonehead might as well be returned to Austin so long as he behaved himself.

Unfortunately, we Texans can no longer count on our legislators to "behave" themselves. As long as the Legislature is in session, our wallets remain in dire jeopardy.

So the Texas Legislature will soon return to Austin to find solutions to other critical issues facing our state.

English-language translation: everyone will have to pay higher taxes.

*****

BODO'S DEER HUNT

One of my best boyhood friends, Bodo Schwamkrug, spent more than his share of time in trouble. It wasn't that Bodo was bad; he just viewed things differently than other people. Deer season, for example, was whenever he wanted deer meat.

Now Bodo knew that there were such things as deer seasons and hunting licenses, but he assumed that they only applied to people who hunted deer for sport. If a person needed fresh venison, he saw nothing wrong with shooting a deer whenever such a need arose. As if that alone wasn't enough to attract the attention of an alert game warden, Bodo also found it most convenient to hunt at night. With a spotlight. From a pickup truck. Along the side of a county road.

Bodo's uncle, Goswin, owned a slaughter house. Since Bodo worked part-time at the slaughter house, he had a set of keys to the place. This came in very handy should Bodo have a pressing need for venison in the middle of the night. Within an hour of one of his midnight roadside hunting trips, Bodo could have the deer skinned, dressed, cut, and wrapped.

For years, Bodo managed to keep his family in meat without difficulty. Then he got greedy. Bodo discovered that there were people who were willing to pay very well for fresh deer meat out of season. The solution seemed simple. Bodo needed cash; the venison connoisseurs needed meat.

His moonlight hunts had been refined into a cunning routine. Bodo would begin preparation in the early evening by putting a large tarp on the bed of his pickup truck, plugging his portable spotlight into the cigarette lighter, and cleaning and loading his favorite .22 rifle.

Bodo preferred the .22 because it didn't make much noise and the shells were inexpensive. He would always shoot the deer in the head (when you spotlight them at night, the deer just stand there and look at you) so none of the valuable meat was lost, making the .22 a very effective deer rifle by his standards.

Sometime after midnight, the undercover hunter would set out to stalk his prey. Bodo knew that none of the sheriff's deputies worked after midnight, so his only concern was the one game warden assigned to the county. On his way to the hunting site, Bodo would drive past the game warden's house. If the officer's car was parked at home, he knew he had nothing to worry about.

Assured of a hassle-free hunt, the twilight deer slayer set out to find a lonely county lane with deer grazing alongside the roadway. Finding his prey, Bodo would train his light on the victim-to-be and quickly dispatch the animal. He would then drag it onto the bed of the truck, cover the evidence-on-the-hoof with the tarp, and head straight to his uncle's slaughter house.

This scheme worked beautifully until the night that Bodo made a little too much noise unloading his prey. A little widow lady lived next door to the slaughter house and, like most little old ladies, resented being awakened by someone rattling around in the middle of the night.

Hearing the noise, the neighbor lady looked out her back window to see a pickup truck pulled up to the back of the business and the rear door standing open. A longtime fan of "Dragnet", the lady immediately knew what was happening. It was a break-in!

Within moments, the police were notified of a burglary-in-progress at the slaughter house. The cops surrounded the place and charged in with guns drawn - just in time to see Bodo hoisting his illegal deer onto a meat hook.

The game warden was notified; the deer and Bodo's rifle were confiscated; and Bodo was put out of business. The Justice of the Peace fined Bodo $50 for illegal hunting.

"But Judge," Bodo pleaded, "that's more than I'd have gotten for selling the meat!"

The judge increased the fine to $75.

Uncle Goswin, not overly happy to have his business used as the scene of the crime, retrieved Bodo's set of keys and put Bodo on "gut duty". It was his job to collect the intestines of the butchered animals, place them in barrels, and take them to the rendering plant.

After about a month on gut duty, Goswin decided to see if Bodo had learned his lesson.

"Well boy," Goswin asked, "you gonna give up illegal hunting?"

"Yes, sir," Bodo beamed. "I've learned my lesson. Besides, I've got a new way to make some pocket money. Instead of hunting, I'm gonna go fishing and sell the fish down at the Catfish Corner Cafe."

"You got a fishing license, boy?" the uncle inquired. "I ain't putting up with illegal fishin' any more than I'll put up with illegal huntin'."

"Sure do, Uncle Goswin," came the reply, "I've got a license, all good and legal. Now all I've got to do is get some dynamite and I'm ready to fish."

*****

COMBAT SCHOOL-BUS DRIVING

About forty years ago, when a Hill Country school district decided to offer school bus transportation to students in isolated rural areas, they knew that they needed to find a very special kind of bus driver.

Since school buses were new to the cedar-covered hills, they needed someone who could handle a noisy group of children while still negotiating treacherous gravel roads with steep grades and hairpin turns. Since county road maps and route addresses were largely unknown, they also needed someone who knew the territory.

Roland Dischinger seemed to fit the bill. He spent World War II driving an ammunition truck for the Army, so he knew how to drive a large vehicle under difficult circumstances. After the war, he spent several years driving the county's only road grader, so he also knew his way around all of the county roads. The school board promptly hired Roland as the district's first bus driver.

What the school board didn't know was that the experience of driving a large, lumbering truck loaded with explosives through combat zones and mine fields had left Roland's nerves completely shot.

Roland, on the other hand, didn't realize how unruly a bus-load of excited little cedar choppers could be. After the first few weeks, he was ready for the comparative peace and quiet of a combat zone.

The first breaking point came one morning when Jeffery Schwarzlose bet Harlon Kraft a new jack-knife that he wouldn't light a firecracker under Sally Ann Startz. Just as Harlon was slipping a Black Cat Super-Popper under Sally, the bus hit a bump and the firecracker slid beneath the driver's seat.

When the explosion went off, Roland's mind instinctively flashed back to the war. In one rapid motion, he slammed the bus to a stop, bailed out and jumped clear. Unfortunately, in his haste to escape the attack, Roland forgot about the fifteen-foot drop just off the edge of the road. He didn't stop rolling until he landed in the shallow water of Kolbe's Creek.

Wet, bruised, and angry, Roland charged back up the hill like Teddy Roosevelt.

"Who did that?" he demanded.

Silence.

"OK, everybody out!" he ordered, "Today, everyone walks to school. The first one to get out of line gets a whipping right here on the side of the road."

And walk they did. An orderly line of dejected delinquents were marched to school with Roland following behind in the bus. That was the end of trouble - at least for a while.

After the spring planting, the Jentsch boys came back to school. The Jentsches only went to school when there was no work to be done around the farm. As a result, all three brothers were in the seventh grade despite the fact that they were

16, 18, and 19 years old.

It was a beautiful spring day, and the boys were less than thrilled with the idea of going to school. They figured that a day of lazing in the sun and swimming in Bear Creek would more suit their needs. There was only one problem; the truants-to-be lacked transportation. Arnold, the oldest of the three, came up with the solution - Roland's school bus.

The Jentsch boys were waiting along Crane's Mill Road just before Roland's first pick-up point. They furiously flagged the bus down as it approached. Roland pulled to a stop and opened the door.

"Hey, Roland," Arnold called out, "your front tire here's going flat."

As Roland stepped out to investigate, the other two brothers grabbed him, removed his pants and boots, and tied him to a cedar tree. All three Jentsches then jumped in the bus and drove off for a day of recreation, courtesy of Roland and the local school system.

After an hour of struggling with the ropes, Roland freed himself and made his way to the nearest house, the home of the widow Meckel. Emma Meckel was working in her garden when she spotted the half-naked bus driver approaching. She immediately grabbed her shotgun and held what she thought was a sex-crazed maniac at bay until the sheriff arrived.

Roland explained his situation to the sympathetic lawman.

"Well, Roland, looks like you've had quite a day," the sheriff told him, "I'll just drive you back to the school."

"I'd appreciate a ride, Sheriff," Roland replied, "but if it's all the same, I'd rather go back to the courthouse with you."

"What in the world do you want at the courthouse?"

"I figured I'd go see the man at the draft board about re-enlisting in the Army," Roland explained, "It's a hell of a lot safer than driving a school bus."

*****

TO SCHWARTZ, OR NOT TO SCHWARTZ ...

Not long ago, I introduced my newspaper readers to Emma and Otto Schwartz and the unfortunate circumstances surrounding the christening of their new outhouse. A kind reader questioned whether I had misspelled Emma and Otto's last name, suggesting that their name should be spelled S-c-h-w-a-r-z instead of S-c-h-w-a-r-t-z.

Realizing that only people of extremely high intelligence, outstanding moral fiber, and exquisite good taste read and appreciate my column, I knew that this was a serious situation. Faced with the prospect of having made the first mistake of my entire life, I was determined to meet this challenge. To Schwartz, or not to Schwartz ...that was the question!

My first source was Ma Bell. I checked as many Hill Country telephone books as I could find - Boerne, Fredericksburg, Blanco, New Braunfels, and Kerrville. I found numerous listings for both Schwartz and Schwarz.

I then figured that counting the variations might be helpful. The final figure was Schwartz-28; Schwarz-25. A slight edge to Schwartz, but too close to call a clear winner. And which was correct for Emma and Otto? The only way to resolve this matter was to go straight to the source.

I decided to drop in and visit Emma and Otto to put the question to rest. I found Otto out behind the chicken coop, working on his tractor.

"Otto, a question has been raised about how you spell your name," I said, "I figured that you could help me out."

"Heck," he laughed, "that's easy. It's O-t-t-o."

"No, no, not your first name. I meant your family name."

"That's tough," Otto pondered as he scratched his chin. "We got eight kids, and they all got different names. There's Ottmar, Hilmar, Erhart, Hilda, Elwin, Hanno, Frieda, and Zina."

"Zina?"

"Well, Emma was hooked on a soap opera at the time. She named our youngest after that actress, Zina Bethune."

"Otto, you're not following me." I explained. "The question is about how you spell your last name. Is it S-c-h-w-a-r-t-z, or is it S-c-h-w-a-r-z?"

"Oh, well that's easy," Otto responded. "Emma and I spell it S-c-h-w-a-r-t-z. Far as I know, all the kids spell it the same way except maybe for Hanno. He never could spell very good, so there's no telling how he spells it."

I was vindicated. This was proof positive that 9 out of 10 Schwartzes in Emma and Otto's family spelled their last name the same way I had.

I then explained how the question arose, and about those who used the S-c-h-w-a-r-z spelling.

"We used to know some folks who spelled their name like that," Otto informed me. "They used to live over toward Sisterdale. They invited me and Emma over to supper one time, but I don't think that we hit it off."

"What happened?" I asked.

"I think it had to do with their dog's water bowl. You see, that water bowl looked an awful lot like one of them fancy spittoons Walter Jentsch has down at the barber shop. Well, nobody told me different, so I spit my chew into it before eating, just like proper folks ought to. It was an honest mistake, but they acted like we were some kind of hillbillies after that."

Otto went on to explain that he had observed other differences between Schwarzes and Schwartzes:

If a Schwarz tears a perfectly-good pair of overalls, he thinks nothing of going out and buying a new pair at a fancy store like K-Mart - if a Schwartz tears a perfectly-good pair of overalls, he will sew a patch on using the first available feed sack.

A Schwarz will join a country club and

play golf on Wednesdays and Sundays - a Schwartz will join a bowling club and play nine-pin on Saturday night.

A Schwarz will buy a new pickup truck when the old one is paid off in four or five years - a Schwartz expects a pickup truck to last twenty years or 200,000 miles, whichever comes first.

A Schwarz gets his hair trimmed and styled at a salon for $20 - a Schwartz gets his hair cut at a barber shop with a striped pole out front for $5.

A Schwarz may openly endorse a Democratic candidate for public office - a Schwartz may vote for a Democrat, but would never admit it, even if tortured.

A Schwarz will join the Rotary Club - a Schwartz will join the Hermann Sons Lodge.

"Oh, there's one other thing," Otto called out to me as I was leaving. "Schwarzes are the ones who like to correct other folks."

I should have known that one.

*****

FRIDAY NIGHT FEVER

As Autumn returns to the Texas Hill Country, the fever begins to spread across the land. No one is immune, and the only known cure is found every Friday night down at the local high school stadium. It's high school football time in Texas.

Texans take their high school football seriously. Bankers, doctors, and business professionals will jam into the stands alongside janitors, farmers, and cedar-choppers one night a week with a singular purpose - to pull for the home team. People who wouldn't otherwise speak to one another in public can be found hugging in jubilation as their team scores the winning touchdown.

Visitors from other states watch in amazement as we Texans adorn ourselves in the school colors, pin on forty or fifty spirit ribbons, and yell for our team until the veins in our necks stand out. It surprises them that a Texan will travel hundreds of miles, crepe-paper streamers adorning the car's antenna, to attend a homecoming game at a high school they attended forty years earlier.

I've always felt somehow left out when the football frenzy hits. Don't get me wrong, I love football. I'm a member of the booster club. I have a pass that lets me watch the game from the sidelines. I can recite the team's record from memory. It's just that, every now and again, I remember my old high school team - the Fighting Unicorns of New Braunfels High.

Yes, Unicorns. Not just plain Unicorns, but Fighting Unicorns. Unfortunately, a Unicorn just doesn't conjure up a fighting image. Unicorns are usually pictured romping playfully around in a pastoral setting with rainbows and waterfalls.

Even our hand sign was pitiful. The University of Texas Longhorns had the "Hook'em

Horns" sign. The Aggies "Gig'em" was a thumb gesture. The Unicorn sign was an upraised right hand with the pinky extended - not exactly the kind of gesture to strike fear in the hearts of your opponent.

Just as the Unicorn is a mythical beast, our ability on the gridiron was equally mythical. We were the team that everyone wanted to play for homecoming. Since everyone wants to win their homecoming game, we became very popular homecoming opponents since just about anyone could beat the Unicorns. One year, just about everyone did.

Our opening game of the season was against the Tivy Antlers. Since they had a name almost as silly as ours, we felt pretty confident. We lost, 24 - 0.

A weak opener, the coaches said, but we were still working out some kinks in the offense and "fine tuning" parts of our game. Next week would be better.

It was - for the other team. We lost to the Fredericksburg Billies 40 - 0. It was bad enough to lose by 40 points, but losing to a team named after a billy-goat was just plain humiliating.

After every Fredericksburg touchdown, the Billie fans would bleat goat sounds at us. To this day, my face turns red every time I hear a goat.

It just couldn't get worse, we thought. We were wrong. The Churchill Chargers devastated us by a score of 64 - 0.

Three weeks into the schedule, and our opponents had outscored us by 128 points. We were yet to score our first point. The coaches stopped talking to the local newspaper and spent a lot of time locked in their offices with the blinds drawn.

Week Four was probably the lowest point of the season, as we faced perennial powerhouse Roosevelt High on their home turf. The Rough Riders destroyed us 72 - 0. I could swear that, by the fourth quarter, they were resting all of their players and had sent their baton twirlers in to play against us.

After the Roosevelt loss, the grumbling in the community was becoming a roar. We were the laughing-stock of the Hill Country. One long-time athletic booster suggested we disband the football team, tear down the stadium, and build a hockey rink. Since no other high school in Texas had a hockey team, we'd be certain state champs.

The rest of the season was equally grim, as we managed to continue to lose every single game. One of the season's few high points was when, in Game Five, we finally scored three points on a field goal against San Marcos. It made front-page headlines in the local paper despite the fact that we lost the game.

The final game of the season was a rainy, sloppy affair against the Huskies of Holmes High. The field was a quagmire, as a cold drizzle fell throughout the game. Both teams were plagued by fumbles and falls.

By the final quarter, we were tied 6 - 6. It actually looked as though we would be able to salvage a tie. Then the miracle occurred.

With less than two minutes left in the game,

the Holmes quarterback fumbled the ball. As both teams slogged and stumbled across the muddy field after the loose pigskin, the ball was kicked backward. Finally, a Holmes player fell on the football just as one of our players fell on him.

The stadium fell into a stunned silence as the referee's whistle blew. They were in the end zone - the Holmes end zone. The Fighting Unicorns had fallen onto a two-point safety. Final score: Holmes Huskies 6 - New Braunfels Fighting Unicorns 8.

The Unicorn faithful erupted into a celebration frenzy. The principal kissed the vice-principal - twice. Cheerleaders cried with joy. The team celebrated by rolling around on the sloppy field. The Unicorns were finally winners.

For that season, our only moment in the sun was, instead, a roll in the mud. It made no difference; it was still a win. The thrill of victory had eclipsed the agony of defeat.

Go Team!

*****

COUNTY FAIR

*"Sunday at the fair can make a memory
more valuable than gold...
'specially when you're ten years old"*

*Roger Miller's
"Tom Green County Fair"*

Every year, as Summer drifted toward Autumn, county fair time rolled around. County fair - a wonderland of spinning, whirling neon lights stretching skyward from the dusty earth below. The faintly exotic smell of grilled burgers and cotton candy mixed with the odor of the diesel engines that powered the carnival kingdom. Polka music from the beer garden provided background for the carnival barkers: "Three balls for a quarter! Everyone's a winner! Who's next?"

It was a time of magic; a time to suspend reality. The children could forget about having to return to school. Instead, they could "ride all the rides" with their red, yellow, and green lights dancing across the fairground skies. The youngsters could devour candied apples and hot dogs until the excitement and fatigue overwhelmed them.

Young men could spend a week's pay to display their prowess by throwing baseballs at stacked milk bottles in an effort to win a stuffed animal for their lady-love. The rodeo fans could watch an endless array of cowboys test their abilities against the broncs and bulls, with the livestock typically emerging victorious.

The ladies could admire, or envy, the handiwork of others as they closely inspected the blue-ribbon winners in the canning and baking contests. They could then reassure themselves, and anyone else who would listen, that they could easily have won first place if they "just had the time" to enter.

The next stop would be a visit to the commercial booths. Here, they could examine first-hand the latest miracle appliances for the farm and home, while listening to fast-pitch salesmen extolling the virtues of their product.

The men would often stroll through the livestock exhibits and take a few minutes to talk with the county agent, who always seemed to be present in the stock barns. There was also the chance to admire the latest in tractors and farm implements, even though there was never enough money to actually consider buying.

As day faded, the evening blues deepened and the colorful lights gave renewed life to the weary fair-goers. The band would summon everyone to the sawdust-covered dance floor for an evening of polkas and waltzes. There, like a couple of teenagers, Oma and Opa would dance the evening away only pausing long enough for Opa to "cut the dust" with a beer.

Finally, as the sound of the last polka drifted across a sea of weary celebrants, and the brilliant lights of the midway yielded to the dark of the night, it was time to leave. The magic that was county fair was over for another year.

But there would always be a next year. And there would always be the kid in someone who would live for another chance to "ride all the rides."

"Time to go. The pickup truck, it rattles down the gravel road. All of us kids sit backwards, looking through the dust clouds at the lights and the laughter at the Tom Green County Fair."

*****

TRICK OR TREAT

Beware. As the first winds of Fall begin blowing across the cedar-covered hillsides, the ghouls and goblins will begin to stir. You'd better be ready for them.

It will be time to stock up on candy and goodies, carve a jack-o-lantern, and wait for the sound of "trick or treat" from marauding Halloween spooks. Unfortunately, Halloween just isn't what it used to be.

Like so many traditions, Halloween is falling by the wayside as a victim of modern society. Fearful for the safety of the children, many communities have discouraged door-to-door trick-or-treating in favor of organized events.

When I was growing up in the Hill Country, there weren't many opportunities to trick-or-treat. The closest neighbor was a brisk ten-minute walk down the road. The time and distance involved just didn't make the effort worthwhile.

On a couple of occasions, Oma and Opa drove me into town so I could go trick-or-treating with Frieda Nolte, the granddaughter of their close friends. While Oma and Opa visited with the Noltes, Frieda and I made our Halloween rounds in her neighborhood.

I was never particularly fond of going with Frieda because she would always introduce me as her boyfriend, and because she always wore a ballerina costume. My favorite costume was a Confederate soldier, and the two just looked silly together. But, free candy was hard to come by, so I never really fought the idea.

After I was forced to wear a particularly-humiliating chicken costume for a school play, I vowed to never go trick- or-treating again. I kept that vow until I was 17 years old, when my best boyhood friend, Bodo Schwamkrug, called and asked me to go with him.

"Bodo, we're both a little too old to go trick-or- treating," I reminded him. "Besides, ever since I had to wear that chicken costume in third grade . . ."

"I know, I know," Bodo interrupted. "I'm not asking you to dress up or anything, I just want you to go with me while I take Harlon."

Harlon was Bodo's 4-year-old brother. Having spent virtually all of his life on the farm,

Harlon knew almost nothing about Halloween or trick-or-treating. In fact, he wasn't totally sold on the idea of dressing up like a ghost and walking up to the homes of complete strangers, even if they were supposed to give him candy.

After some negotiating, in which Bodo promised to tune-up my car and pay me the ten dollars he owed me, I reluctantly agreed to go along.

At first, Harlon refused to go near the houses unless Bodo and I went along. After the first block, however, his caution was replaced by out-and-out greed. He literally raced ahead of the other juvenile goblins to make sure he got his share of candy. Everything went smoothly until he reached the door of Miss Emily Krueger.

What none of us knew at the time was how much Miss Krueger loved Halloween. She loved it so much that she would dress up like a witch, complete with green make-up and fake warts, and answer the door cackling and screaming like something out of the "Wizard of Oz".

Harlon bounded up the walk, carefully adjusted his costume, and rang the door bell. No sooner had he opened his mouth to shout "trick or treat" than Miss Krueger whipped open the door.

"Ah, ha, ha, ha, my pretty," the faux-witch screamed. "You'd make a fine, plump Halloween treat."

Harlon froze with fear and stared in panic at the apparition before him.

"Well, little boy? Wouldn't you like to try some of my apples?" the witch said as she offered a candy apple.

Faced with what he was certain was a poisoned apple, little Harlon dropped his bag of candy, turned, and ran screaming out of the yard. And past me. And past his brother. And down the street. And out of sight.

Bodo and I searched for an hour. We checked every tree, bush, and drain culvert in a ten-block area. Harlon was nowhere to be found.

Resigned to the fact that we had to go home and tell Bodo's mother that we had misplaced her youngest son, we trudged back to Bodo's truck.

As we walked up, we heard sniffling sounds coming from the back of the pickup. Bodo pulled back some feed sacks and, sure enough, we found the horrified little hobgoblin's hiding place.

"Don't let the witch get me!" Harlon sobbed.

"Harlon, that's no real witch," Bodo assured him. "Sometimes adults get dressed up on Halloween. It was just a kind of joke."

Harlon thought for a second and then broke out crying again.

"For pete's sake, what's wrong now?" Bodo asked.

"I lost all my candy, and it wasn't even a real witch," Harlon bawled.

Desperate to halt Harlon's wailing, Bodo stopped at the witch's house to see if, by some miracle, the bag of candy was still there. He walked up to the porch and looked around, but no goodies were to be found.

Just as he was turning to leave, the door opened. The witch, minus her make-up, was standing there holding Harlon's bag of candy. In fact, the bag of candy seemed much larger than before.

Miss Krueger walked up to the truck and offered the candy to Harlon.

"I'm sorry I frightened you before," the ex-sorceress said as she smiled. "You see, I just enjoy Halloween so much that I sometimes get carried away. I don't mean to really scare anyone."

As Harlon returned the smile, we knew that Harlon Schwamkrug's first Halloween had been saved by the Witch of Commerce Street.

Today when I think about Halloween, I remember Emily Krueger. She was one of those special people who never lost her joy for life, or her sense of humor. She wasn't about to let Halloween be just for kids. Life was just too much fun to become old and bitter.

Maybe if we all could have a sense of humor; maybe if we all could have a slightly cock-eyed view of our world; maybe if we all could laugh at ourselves a little more easily; maybe then we could re-capture some of those "good old days" we all seem to be yearning for.

Maybe this year, I'll go trick-or-treating again.

*****

OMA

Oma celebrated her 79th birthday last week. Although she's never achieved fame or fortune as defined by most people, she is - in my eyes - one of the greatest people who ever lived.

Oma was born Norma Bertha Jentsch in the small Hill Country hamlet of Sattler on October 24, 1912. She was born into a world that would be considered primitive by today's standards.

The Hill Country of 1912 had no paved roads, automobiles, telephones, indoor plumbing, electricity, or any of the other modern conveniences that we take for granted today. The entire family, children included, worked in the fields to eke out a bare living from the hardscrabble earth.

Education came in a one-room schoolhouse, with all grades being taught together. Too often, farm kids like Oma could only attend school when they weren't needed for work at home. Despite these hardships, Oma achieved greatness.

No, she didn't win civic awards, become a millionaire, cure a dreaded disease, or become a well-known media celebrity. She achieved greatness by touching the lives of others.

She managed to raise two sons by herself after her first husband left. Both sons went on to become well-respected professionals and made good lives for themselves.

Some 40-odd years ago, she met and married her second husband, James Thompson - Opa, as we call him. They have stayed together, through good times and bad, and are still happily married today.

Some thirty years ago, after working for others all their lives, Oma and Opa decided to start their own business - a small upholstery shop. Through hard work and honesty, the little shop prospered, while Oma and Opa's reputation for treating customers like family spread throughout the Hill Country.

In 1956, Oma and Opa decided to raise a grandson. Because of a series of family misfortunes, the little one's parents weren't able to take care of him. At a time in their lives when they should have started thinking about the "good life" instead of worrying about raising a kid, Oma and Opa took me in.

Oma was always there for me. When my class at Lamar Elementary School needed a "room mother" to help out, she was always the first volunteer. When my Cub Scout pack needed a Den Mother, she took the job.

At every school play, band concert, parent's night, or anything else that I was involved in, she was there. That was often after, or before, putting a full day's work in at the upholstery shop. No matter how tired, or how busy, or how overwhelmed with other things she might have been, Oma was always there.

Whenever I marched in a parade, she stood in the hot sun to watch and take pictures. When I wanted to go trick-or-treating but couldn't because we lived in the country, she took me in to town and went with me from door to door. Whenever I wasn't feeling well, she sat with me and told me stories.

It was only after I was out on my own that Oma and Opa could truly make time for themselves. They started taking vacations. They bought things to make their lives a little easier. They could go out to dinner or to socialize with friends.

In 1976, Oma had a stroke. After weeks of hospitalization and rehabilitation, she bounced back. The only lasting effect of the stroke was a slight weakness in her left leg.

In 1984, it happened again. After the second stroke, she had to rely on a cane to get around because her "bad leg" became even weaker. Oma's spirit, however, was not diminished and she wasn't about to slow down any more than she absolutely had to.

Today, Oma supervises the others at work in the upholstery shop. Opa still works in the shop as well, because he likes to keep busy. When not overseeing shop operations, Oma likes to sit in her favorite rocking chair and read as her cat, Gilbert, sleeps at her feet.

She still enjoys summer meals of watermelon and butter bread. She enjoys reading mystery novels. She is the kind of person who enjoys the simple pleasures of Hill Country life.

So when they pass out the great awards of achievement or "Citizen of the Year" plaques, Oma won't be a recipient. Her accomplishments won't be found on the front page of the newspaper or covered on the evening newscast. She has done her life's work in a simpler, more human, fashion.

She has profoundly touched the lives of others and, in doing so, has made their lives better. She has done this through her quiet strength, her simple ways, her determined resolve, her limitless compassion, and her enduring love. I know this because mine is one of those lives she has touched.

Happy Birthday, Oma. I love you.

*****

WINTER IN THE HILL COUNTRY

*****

AGAPITO'S PIG

A Comal County jury recently convicted the owner of a Vietnamese potbellied pig of violating an ordinance that prohibits the keeping of swine within the city limits. The owner insisted that her pig was not a "hog" as defined in the ordinance, but was, instead, a house pet.

Citing the county's legal position, the assistant county attorney stated, "A hog is sort of like pornography. You know one when you see one."

Upon reading this masterful piece of legal logic, I couldn't help but recall Agapito Flores and his pet pig, Maria Elena. Agapito was devoted to his pig, and the pig was equally loyal to her master. Agapito would probably have been offended to hear someone compare Maria Elena with pornography.

Agapito lived just outside of Gruene, Texas, in a small farmhouse. He had worked all his life as a hand on the Kaderli ranch. When Agapito got older, the Kaderli family gave him the small wooden-frame home on a plot of property near the main ranch house. Here, the old ranch hand could live out his golden years in relative comfort, tending his garden while still doing light chores around the ranch.

Maria Elena became attached to Agapito when she was just a piglet. While still quite small, she had wandered away from the litter and had fallen into an abandoned well. Hearing the frantic squealing, Agapito rigged a net on the end of a long rope and snared the helpless pig. From that day forward, they were inseparable. Agapito decided to name the pig after a maiden aunt.

"My aunt was a very round woman," he would say. "When I first saw this little pig with her round face, round body, and short little legs, I thought of my aunt. Maria Elena was a good name for my aunt, so I figured it's a pretty good name for my pig, too."

The little pig followed the old ranch hand everywhere. When Agapito went into the pastures to fix a fence or search for a lost calf, Maria Elena would chase along behind him as fast as her little legs would allow. After the day's work was done, the pig would follow him home.

At first, Agapito wouldn't let the pig into the house. She would sleep on the porch, right next to the door. As the months and years passed, Maria Elena was occasionally allowed inside. Eventually, she became a permanent tenant, sleeping behind the wood stove.

When Agapito got too old to work in the pastures, he would spend the days tending his garden as Maria Elena watched from the porch. When Agapito took his daily walk along Hunter Road, the pig would follow along like a faithful dog.

During the warm summer evenings, Agapito liked to walk to Crenwelge's Ice House for a cool beer and some friendly conversation. Naturally, Maria Elena came along and laid in a quiet corner while her master visited. Mr. Crenwelge, after some initial reluctance, accepted the pig and even started saving small scraps of food as treats for Maria Elena.

Only one customer, Henry Hardemann, ever complained. Hardemann ran a junkyard and stopped by the ice house every evening on his way home.

"Hey, Crenwelge," the irritated Hardemann hollered when he first spotted Maria Elena, "what's that filthy pig doing in here?"

"That pig looks and smells a lot better than you do," Crenwelge shot back, "and if you don't like it, you can try to find someplace else where they'll let you drink on credit until payday."

Hardemann thought about it for a second and realized that Crenwelge had a point. There probably was no one else who would let him run a tab until he made enough money to pay for his thirst.

"Well, I guess she is pretty clean for a pig," Hardemann finally said. "Besides, she kind of reminds me of a girl I dated in high school."

"Girl was probably too good for him," the ice-house keeper mumbled under his breath as the junk man ordered a round of beer for the house - on credit, of course.

The friendship between Agapito and Maria Elena lasted for many years. One dark morning, the old man found his pet laying on the floor near the back door. The pig was so sick that she couldn't move except to raise her head and stare mournfully at her lifelong friend. The old man tried every home-cure he could think of, but could do nothing to help. By nightfall, Maria Elena was gone.

The next day, Agapito buried Maria Elena alongside his small garden. He fashioned a tiny wooden marker, offered a prayer, and said goodbye.

The old man lovingly planted flowers around Maria Elena's grave, cultivating the little plot of ground as carefully as his garden. One day, Mr. Kaderli asked Agapito why he spent so much time tending the grave of a pet.

"Most people don't think much of a pig, but Maria Elena was my good friend," the old man explained. "Her company made me happy the same way flowers make me happy. It just seemed right for this to be a place that I could look at and still feel happy."

If Agapito were alive today, he probably wouldn't understand all the fuss over a pet pig.

*****

A MODERN-DAY DINOSAUR

The Geezinslaw Brothers have a song that says it best: I'm a dinosaur. In fact, it was a trip to the music store to buy just such a record that began to make it quite clear that I probably fit into the dinosaur category.

Walking into the record store, I quickly realized that something was missing. There were no records. There were cassette tapes, compact discs, laser discs, and videotapes, but absolutely no records.

Apparently seeing my confusion, a store clerk walked up and asked if I needed any help. The clerk was a young lady, about 17 years old, with orange hair. She was dressed like she had put her underwear on outside of her clothes.

"Where are your records?" I asked.

"Our what?" she asked with a puzzled look on her face.

"Records," I explained. "You know, those

things with recorded music on them."

The puzzled look on the girl's face didn't change.

"Records; albums. They're flat, black, round, and plastic," I patiently continued. "You put them on your stereo turntable and it makes music."

"Oh, wow," she replied. "You, like, want an antique store, right? This is a music store."

"No, I don't want to buy 78's," I said, my voice rising. "I want to buy an album."

"What are 78's?" she asked as the puzzled expression returned. "And albums you've got to get at the photo shop. Like I said, man, this is a music store."

It was painfully obvious that one of us was in the wrong place. Since I was the only one in the shop that didn't seem to know what was going on, I thanked the girl and left. I think she called mall security and reported me as some sort of weirdo.

To be quite honest with you, it came as a shock to me to find out that they don't make record albums anymore. A quick look at my record collection will bear out the fact that I haven't bought a lot of records since the early 1970's.

When "disco" arrived, I tuned my radio to an all-talk station and left it there. If I really feel the need to listen to music, I drag out my old Beatles, Chicago, or Creedence Clearwater Revival albums.

I know that 45's went by the wayside some years ago. That's why I have my cherished copy of "Johnny Angel" - by the lovely and talented Shelley Fabares - locked away in my safe for protection. But, somehow, nobody told me that the album had followed the 78 and the 45 to that great record-bin in the sky.

Disappointed, I got into my car to go home for lunch. Once again, modern technology hit me in the face.

I've had my new car for about six months now, but I still haven't figured out how to set the digital clock in the dashboard. Every time I drive, I have to look at the wrong time, flashing at me like a beacon and telling the world that I don't know how the clock works.

The car even has all kinds of electronic gadgets, including a little voice to tell me when to fasten my seat belts and turn off my headlights. You would think that a car that smart ought to be able to set its own damn clock.

When I got home for lunch, I found myself up against another modern miracle that I haven't mastered - the microwave oven. My wife just bought this new microwave with a control panel that looks like the command console in the space shuttle. The instruction manual looks like an encyclopedia.

I decided to experiment and try to heat up a chicken pot-pie in this little nuclear menace. After twenty minutes of trying, all I could get the thing to do was beep at me. By this time, the pot-pie had thawed on its own, so I gave it to the dog and drove to the Fat Cat Cafe for a burger.

As I was eating, my good friend Bodo Schwamkrug came in carrying a wristwatch.

"Hey, John. Can you help me with my new watch?" he asked as he sat down. "I can't seem to figure out how to set the time."

"Just pull out the stem and move the hands clockwise, Bodo," I explained.

"Hands? This thing don't have no hands," he said, showing me a digital watch with about fifteen little buttons on it.

"What happened to your old watch?" I asked.

"Oh, nothing. I just saw this one down at the Wal-Mart and figured I needed something more modern," my friend explained. "With these little buttons, I can set an alarm to go off, use it as a stopwatch, and even find out what time it is in Paris."

"Sorry, Bodo. I can't help you," I told him. "Technology's just not my thing. Besides, why would you care what time it is in Paris?"

"Get with it, John," Bodo urged. "This is the 1990's. You've got to keep up with the times."

Disappointed with the turn of the day's events, I returned home to the sound of the ringing phone. It was my beloved newspaper editor, telling me that they needed my column - pronto.

Again, it would be me against modern technology. The fastest way to get my column in to the newspaper office was to fax it.

"We always get a kick out of it when you fax your column in," the editor explained to me. "You always send it to us upside-down."

Perfect, I thought to myself. It's bad enough that it usually takes me three or four tries to get the fax machine to work. Now I find out that, all this time, I've been sending fax messages upside-down.

"Well, you know how it is," I grumbled. "Everyone's got to have his own style."

I faxed my column in. Upside-down. On purpose. I even enjoyed it. It was like thumbing my nose at technology.

Like the Geezinslaw Brothers' song says: I'm a dinosaur. It's just my style.

*****

MRS. DAVIS' SUNDAY SCHOOL LESSON

Hettye Davis was in her nineties when I first met her. She lived with her daughter and son-in-law, Juanita and Don McCollister, in a sprawling ranch-style home out in the country. She was as independent in her nineties as most of us are in our twenties, and she proved it one Sunday morning by catching a burglar single-handed.

Although a devout Baptist all her life, Hettye had been feeling a little under the weather and decided to stay home while everyone else went to church. Her daughter was concerned about leaving Hettye alone because there had been a rash of burglaries in the area. In fact, the break-ins had been something of a local mystery since the local sheriff could never figure out how

"If I'm not old enough to stay home by myself, I don't know who is." Hettye stubbornly insisted. "I'll be just fine."

She stayed; they went.

After about thirty minutes, Hettye heard something unusual - noises on the roof. Then, she noticed soot falling into the fireplace. She instantly realized that it was the burglar, and he was coming down the chimney!

Hettye rushed to the closet, grabbed a shotgun, and waited at the fireplace for the uninvited visitor.

"I hear you up there," Hettye hollered up the chimney, "and if you show yourself in my fireplace and you ain't Santa Claus, I'm gonna meet you with both barrels of my shotgun."

While the burglar in the chimney probably didn't know it, Hettye knew her way around a shotgun. She liked to pass the time on quiet days sitting by the stock tank and shooting water moccasins. In earlier days she used a .22 rifle to dispatch the snakes, but as she got older, her aim was not quite as accurate. That was when she switched to a shotgun.

Hearing Hettye's challenge, the thief decided to make a hasty retreat. Momentary silence was followed by rapid movement from within the chimney. Soot dropped into the fireplace as the burglar hurriedly attempted to scratch his way back up the chimney - then silence.

"Help me," a voice plaintively called from within the fireplace. "I'm stuck in here."

"Suppose I shoot up that chimney," Hettye called back, "think that'll help you along?"

"No, really. I can't move. I tried to turn around and get back out, but now I'm stuck," the voice pleaded.

Not entirely convinced of the felon's sincerity, Hettye decided she needed a plan to keep the burglar in place until the authorities could get there. She began to stack firewood in the fireplace.

"What are you doing?" the voice cried.

"Nothing for you to worry about unless you try to move," Hettye told the trapped criminal as she splashed kerosene across the firewood. "But if you try to move, up or down, I'm lighting this fire."

Assured of the burglar's complete cooperation, Hettye telephoned the sheriff to inform him that she had a criminal in custody.

"There's no big rush, he's not going anywhere," she told the astonished lawman, "but I'd appreciate it if you could come by and pick him up before I need to use the fireplace. The smoke would back up in the house something terrible."

Don and Juanita returned just as the sheriff was arriving.

"Mother! What in the world is wrong?" Juanita asked as she rushed into the home.

Hettye explained her capture of the crook as the rascal's cries filtered down the chimney. As it turned out, this was the same person who had been burglarizing homes in the area, and he had been coming down chimneys to get in. His scheme had been successful until he ran into Hettye Davis.

"Don and the sheriff had to go up on the

roof, let down a rope, and pull him out," Hettye laughed as she told me the story sometime later. "For a while I thought about lighting that fire. Then I thought about just leaving him stuck in there. But, either way, he would have smelled up the whole house."

"So, since it was Sunday," she grinned, "and he should have been in church, I figured he needed to be reminded of a Sunday-school lesson."

The lesson?

"Thou Shalt Not Steal."

*****

PANNAS - BREAKFAST OF CHAMPIONS

Have you seen the television commercial with Boomer ("You'd better not call me Norman") Esiason, Cincinnati Bengals quarterback, touting Wheaties? Esiason is just the latest of many professional athletes to credit Wheaties - "Breakfast of Champions" - for their physical prowess and athletic success. I can't help but wonder what would have happened if, instead of Wheaties, these super-jocks had been raised on breakfasts of pannas.

In years past, many Hill Country kids, especially those of German heritage, were awakened - no jolted - from bed by the smell of frying pannas. These are the same kids who did two hours of chores every morning; walked a mile or more to school; attended class; walked back home; and then worked on the farm until past sundown. I wonder if they could have done all of that on a cereal breakfast?

Often, these kids ate only two meals a day - breakfast and supper. Schools didn't offer a lunch program and students were on their own for a noon meal. Some brought a modest snack, often just a sweet potato, while others simply did without. Breakfast was expected to carry you through until suppertime.

Now I know there are some people who will smile upon being reminded of pannas. Others will cringe. Still others will wonder just what the heck pannas is. Well, if Wheaties is the "Breakfast of Champions", pannas is the "Breakfast of Cedar-Choppers."

Pannas is a pork dish, sort of. When a family butchered a pig, pannas was made from some of the left-overs. Remnants such as the head, ears, skin, liver, and heart were put into a large outdoor caldron and cooked with water. This concoction was stirred, preferably with a reasonably-clean two-by-four, as it was heated. The broth portion of the hot mixture would then be drained off to make the pannas.

The solids that remained were used to make blood sausage and head cheese. In case you didn't know it, Hill Country folks have a reputation for being somewhat frugal, even when butchering. No part of the pig was thrown away except the squeal.

Once drained, the pannas broth was then

brought inside, placed in a smaller pot, and mixed with a small portion of ground meat. To this, cornmeal (with a little touch of flour) was slowly added until the desired thickness was achieved. After that, everything was poured into a pan to cool and harden.

The final product was a cake of pannas that looked somewhat like a cross between a block of cheese and a roll of breakfast sausage. For breakfast, mama simply sliced off as much pannas as was needed to feed her herd of cedar-choppers and fried it all up in a pan.

Pannas was a true stick-to-your-ribs German meal. You know the kind - food with corners. This was a breakfast that would not only get you through a busy day, but helped keep you "regular" as well. In fact, my grandfather still swears that pannas is the best natural laxative in the world, even better than a bus-station cheeseburger.

Over the years, thousands of acres have been plowed; hundreds of stumps have been pulled; and acres of cedar have been chopped by hearty Germans girded for a hard day's work by a breakfast of pannas. Had there been time for athletics after all of the chores, I wonder how many All-Stars the Hill Country could have produced?

If Michael Jordan of the Chicago Bulls basketball team had been served pannas for breakfast instead of Wheaties, would he be able to score fifty points a game? Would "Air" Jordan be able to slam-dunk from the free throw line?

How about baseball? Would Mark McGwire of the Oakland A's be able to hit sixty home-runs a season after a hearty plate of pannas? Would baseball legend Nolan Ryan be able to throw that 95mph fastball until he is 60 years old?

Would the Cincinnati Bengals be able to win the Super Bowl if they all tanked-up on Pannas instead of Wheaties?

Hey, Boomer. Better eat your pannas.

*****

MAIL-ORDER ALLIGATOR

As a kid growing up in the Hill Country, I was surrounded by all kinds of animals. There was Shorty the pig, Bozo the dog, Oscar the cat, an old turkey-gobbler that I never bothered to name, and a turtle named Roger Maris. There were also assorted chickens, ducks, geese, mules, and rabbits on our little farm. However, the strangest member of our little menagerie came by US Mail.

It was a warm summer afternoon when the telephone rang. It was the local postmaster calling for my grandmother.

"Norma, this is Tug Pfeuffer down at the post office," the postmaster said. "I thought I'd call you about this package we've got down here for John."

"For John?" Oma asked in a surprised tone.

"He's only eight. What kind of package could he have in the mail?"

"That's why I called," came the reply, "the package has air holes in it and says there's a live alligator inside."

"Tug, this telephone line is bad," Oma said. "It sounded like you said alligator."

"That's right, Norma. The package says there's a live alligator in this box," Mr. Pfeuffer responded. "Can you come down here?"

I was laying on a bale of hay in the barn, lazily reading the latest copy of Action Comics, when the still summer air was pierced by the sound of Oma calling my name. I knew that tone well. It was the kind of call that usually meant that I was in trouble.

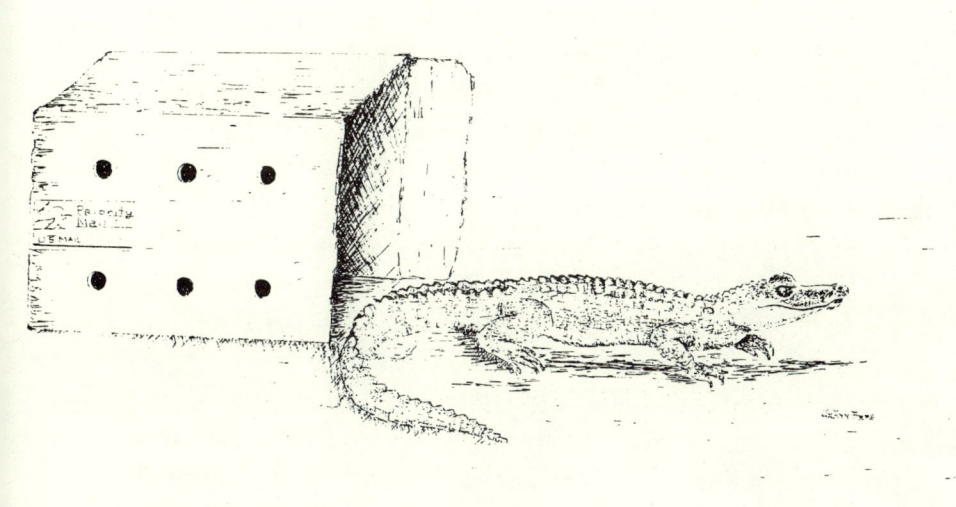

Grabbing my comic, I ran toward the house while trying desperately to remember what kind of indiscretion I might have committed, along with a perfectly good explanation. I was met by Oma with one of those what-have-you-done-this-time looks on her face.

"The postmaster called," she informed me. "He says there's a box with a live alligator in it at the post office for you."

I had become intrigued with alligators after seeing them fed whole chickens at the Alligator Gardens in San Antonio. Quite naturally, I was ecstatic at the prospect of having my very own alligator. Oma, for some reason, didn't seem to share my appreciation of carnivorous reptiles.

"How in the world did you manage to order an alligator by mail?" Oma asked.

I quickly showed her the ad in the back of my comic book: "Hey, Kids! Your Own Alligator - Guaranteed Real and Alive! Only $5."

Now five dollars was big money for a farm kid in the Texas Hill Country. I managed to save the money by scouring the roadsides for returnable soda-pop bottles and cashing them in at Krenwelge's Drive-In. I also skipped lunch at school for several weeks and added that money to my "alligator fund".

After hearing my explanation, Oma reluctantly drove me to town to retrieve my mail-order alligator. I was excited. She, to put it mildly, was not.

Our arrival had been eagerly anticipated at the post office. Mr. Pfeuffer escorted us to the back room where assorted mail-carriers, window clerks, and other postal personnel were examining a small box.

"Might be a good idea to open it here and check," Mr. Pfeuffer suggested as Oma signed for the package. The rest of the crowd, curious to see the contents, eagerly nodded their heads in agreement.

Carefully I opened the box and, to the amazement of everyone but me, inside was a live, six-inch-long alligator. Judging from his cross disposition, he wasn't nearly as impressed with us as we were with him.

I immediately christened my new pet "Al" and bought him a new home from the local Winns' store - one of those little turtle bowls with a plastic palm tree in the middle. Within his dime-store domain, the tiny alligator grew and prospered on a diet of small pieces of hamburger meat. When Al began escaping from the turtle bowl, we moved him into a second-hand aquarium. Over the weeks and months, he continued to grow, devouring more and more hamburger meat.

When the gator grew to over a foot long, it became obvious that something had to be done. Oma convinced me that Al could no longer lead a happy life in a glass aquarium. Besides, alligators over a foot long just don't make good house pets.

Late one night, we packed Al into the truck, drove him to a secluded spot on the Comal River, and gave him his freedom. My five-dollar alligator slipped silently into the darkness.

We never saw the alligator after that, and I've always wondered what became of him. Did he make his way downstream, or does he still live in some quiet back-wash of the Comal? If so, does he resent all those folks in inner-tubes floating down his river? Does he miss those meals of hamburger meat?

I suppose if we ever hear about some tourist disappearing after tubing down the Comal River while eating a Big Mac, maybe we will know what happened to the mail-order alligator of Comal County.

*****

RAMBO MEETS BAMBI

A recent edition of Texas Game & Fish magazine carried an interesting article. It was written by a very determined lady intent upon bagging a deer that appeared to be equally determined to survive.

After taking several "carefully aimed" shots at the five-point buck with no success, this intrepid female hunter ran out of ammunition. Unwilling to let a trophy escape, she then took off after the deer and beat it with her gun butt. The rifle's stock broke; the deer did not.

The dauntless sportswoman then grabbed her knife and stabbed the poor beast several times, but the blade was apparently too short to do any serious damage. She then attempted to "bulldog" the whitetail and break the creature's neck. Still no luck.

In a final attempt to overwhelm her prey, the woman used the gun strap of her rifle to tie the animal's antlers to a nearby fence. The deer was thus secured while the huntress went back to camp to get enough help to finish off the resilient buck.

When the lady returned with her husband, they found the deer, still tied to the fence, quite dead. My bet is that the poor beast died of humiliation. The only unanswered question is why this woman would publicly disclose her role in this poorly-executed assassination.

Of course, this is not the first example of hand-to-hand combat with a deer that I've heard of. My father once used a similar technique to neutralize a spike buck who was regularly committing indiscretions upon the back patio of his house.

At the time, Dad was living at Medina Lake. The front of his home had a lovely view of the lake while the back side had a large stone patio that backed up to a brushy undeveloped area. My father quickly came to regard the back patio, with it's huge native-stone built-in barbecue pit, as his "special" place.

He came to accept the fact that the raccoons and possums expected their fair share of table scraps. He even tolerated the neighbor's cat coming to sleep in the flower bed. But when an upstart yearling started regularly relieving himself on the patio, that meant war!

The first time he discovered the deer droppings on the patio, Dad simply thought it odd for a usually-reclusive animal to use a patio as a bathroom. He used the garden hose to wash off the mess.

But things didn't stop there. Every morning, a fresh calling card was found at the back door. Every morning, my father hosed down the mess. It didn't take too many morning scrub-down sessions for him to decide that something had to be done.

Dad decided to stake out the scene of the crime and apprehend the culprit. From a darkened kitchen window, he waited - ever vigilant

- until almost 2:00 am. Then, from the darkness he heard a sound. Shortly afterward, a spike buck appeared from the brush. Cautiously, the deer approached as Dad watched from the window.

The young buck made his way up onto the patio, looked around carefully, and backed up to the patio door and did what came naturally. Enraged, my father burst through the door screaming, stepped in the middle of the fresh deer doo-doo, slipped, and fell on top of the smelly pile. As the startled buck retreated into the safety of the underbrush, the lights from the neighboring houses came on to the sound of my father's swearing.

Humiliated, but not defeated, Dad began to plan the next night's strategy. He rigged a large net along the ceiling of the patio with a trip-wire directly over the deer's target area. He then built himself a make-shift blind behind the barbecue pit from which he would cut off the animal's escape route.

By 10:00 pm, my father was concealed and the trap rigged for action. There was nothing to do but wait.

Again, just before 2:00 am, the deer made his way to the patio. As the anxious animal prepared to do his thing, my father dropped the net. The alarmed creature not only relieved himself out of sheer fright, but bolted across the barbecue pit and crashed directly into Dad's hide-out.

A furious fight ensued between Dad and the deer. Dad held the beast around the neck with one arm and grabbed his favorite barbecue fork from the pit. The two fought across the patio and into the underbrush where my father finally prevailed, dispatching the incontinent whitetail with the barbecue fork.

As Dad emerged, dragging his victim behind him, the bright spotlight of a Deputy Sheriff's patrol car illuminated the scene.

"All right, Daniel Boone," the Deputy commanded, "drop the deer and the fork. Don't you know it's illegal to hunt deer out of season - especially with barbecue implements?"

"It's not what it looks like. I wasn't hunting," Dad pleaded. "It was either him or me. It was self defense!"

*****

HOMETOWN RADIO
A BLAST FROM THE PAST

Hometown radio is alive and well in the Texas Hill Country. What is hometown radio? Quite simply, it is radio as it used to be; radio that served to bind a community together.

Forty years ago, when small, low-power AM radio stations were just being established in rural Texas towns, these stations served their listeners in many ways. They provided entertainment, just as their slick counterparts do today, but much of the entertainment was local. You could hear local musicians and high school bands mixed in with the latest songs from Ernest Tubb or Hank Williams.

In German, Czech, and Polish areas, polka music was the programming of choice. Such old favorites as "Whoopie" John Wilfhart, the Six Fat Dutchmen, and the Cloverleafs provided endless hours of toe-tapping merriment.

Every station had local news, usually called something like "Party Line Report". In one case, that name was unusually appropriate. One local radio reporter actually picked up bits of news by listening in on telephone party-line conversations in the evening and then broadcasting the gossip on his news program the next morning.

In short, the local radio station kept everyone entertained and informed.

In recent years, powerful FM stations, with signals beamed across the country-side from larger cities, have caused many local AM operations to fall by the wayside. With it's clear, static-free stereo signal and high-tech compact-disc music, FM radio has become the choice of most radio listeners. Most listeners, but not all.

I was driving through the Hill Country recently and found that, because of the rugged terrain, I couldn't pick up a clear FM signal on my car radio. I switched to AM and hit the "scan" button, hoping to find something entertaining to pass the time. Instead, I found myself in a time warp filled with hometown radio.

The radio locked onto a program called "Polka as You Like It". German Polkas were followed by Czech Polkas and Polish Polkas, all announced by a fellow with a thick German accent.

"What language is that man speaking?" my wife asked.

"It's English," I told her, "he just has a little accent."

"A little accent? I can't understand a word he's saying. And that music sounds like something you'd hear at one of your family's reunions." My wife never had a great appreciation for polka music.

Between the polka pieces, the host passed along dedications and greetings to shut-ins and people in nursing homes. He also told his audience who was sick, who was in the hospital, and who was doing better. Other social notes included the menu at the upcoming Hermann Sons Lodge supper, which polka band would be playing at the Eagle's Hall dance on Saturday night, and the fact that Mrs. Viola Liebscher's daughter was in town for a weekend visit from Houston.

The commercial spots did not feature a slick spokesman or catchy jingles to sell their products. Instead, the announcer with the heavy accent told his listeners about the great deals down at Radtke's Hardware ("Bruno just got in the new seed catalogs, so go down and see him in time for the planting season.") and Fritz' Meat Market ("Fritz has fresh bratwurst almost every day, and homemade pannas.").

When the polka program ended, it was time for the bowling report. By telephone, the manager of the local bowling alley reported on last evening's Ladies' Social-Time Bowling League. He noted that Betty Ludwig picked up a 2-7 split twice, and that Emma Freitag was the overall winner of the event.

Get-well wishes were passed along to a bowler that had been in the hospital. We were all reminded of the upcoming bowling tournament and dance ("You don't have to bowl to dance.") and that lanes were always available for family outings ("We have plenty of lanes open, even during tournaments.").

After the bowling report, our announcer told us that it was time for the afternoon music program. What followed was a mixture of polka music (again), the local high school band playing marches, and country music. All of the country music seemed to have been recorded before 1960, and the announcer took great pride in pointing out which songs were being played from original 78rpm recordings.

As I continued to drive, the hometown radio signal was lost. We had passed through the time warp and had returned to the present. At no time did the station ever identify itself nor the town from which it was broadcasting. I guess they figured that their listeners already knew all of that.

"Where was that station from?" my wife asked.

I'm not sure. Maybe it was from a better time.

*****

A CEDAR-CHOPPER'S CHRISTMAS

'Twas the night before Christmas
and throughout the hills
the wood stoves were crackling
to ward off the chills.

Die Kinder hung stockings
on the post of the bed,
hoping for candy
and not switches, instead.

Asleep in the loft
of our cabin of wood,
the young ones dreamt
of gifts for the good.

"It's Christmas tomorrow,"
Meine Frau softly said.
"Put some wood on the fire
and come on to bed."

When back by the outhouse
there came such a noise,
I thought it'd been tipped over
by those bad Dietert boys.

Out to the porch
I ran with a bound,
tripped over the dog
and fell to the ground.

The moon shone lightly
through the brushes and trees;
the scent of cedar was heavy
in the cool Winter breeze.

I couldn't believe
when I saw what I saw,
walk past the hog pens
and up through the draw.

St. Nicholas, in person
himself, did appear!
"Weinachtsman!" I cried,
"What are you doing here?"

"Like so many," he told me,
"from the east to the west,
I love the Hill Country
above all the rest."

"But my reindeer have trouble
finding places to park.
'Cause the hills are so rocky,
their hooves kick up sparks."

"So, while it may look different,
and it may bend the rules,
when I come to the Hill Country,
I trade reindeer for mules."

By the arm, Santa took me
out behind the shed,
Around Opa's smokehouse,
to his sleigh, I was led.

But pulling the rig
were eight mules in a row,
and one single goat,
with his nose all aglow.

He said, "This is my sled
for the Hill Country route:
fine, sturdy mules and
a goat with a red snout."

He grabbed up his sack,
filled with goodies and toys;
home-made dolls for the girls,
wooden trains for the boys.

Inside the cabin
Nick carefully crept,
not making a sound
as the family all slept.

A string of rock candy
and some nuts and some fruit,
he filled all the stockings
and left extra to boot!

"I'm sorry to rush,
but I've got to go.
Texas is so big
that I just can't be slow."

"There are cabins to visit
from bottom to top;
from Kendalia's homes
to the Bulverde stop."

"I'm going through Boerne,
Comfort and Kyle,
and somewhere past Sattler,
I'll rest for awhile."

"But when it's all over
and my rounds are all done,
the Hill Country children
will have their Christmas fun."

To his sled team he hollered,
"Come on, mules, let's fly."
As the team started forward,
St. Nick waved good-bye.

Into the night
the mule team, they rose,
and the leader, goat Rudolph,
lit up his nose.

I ran to the cabin
and woke up my wife
and told her of the strangest
sight I'd seen in my life.

Meine Frau looked disgusted,
"Well, isn't this fine!
Christmas Eve, and you're drunk
on Agarita wine."

So remember this Christmas,
if you see Santa Claus,
before you tell someone
you might stop and pause.

Disbelievers abound,
they'll think that you're tight,
if you see jolly elves
and mule teams at night.

But hold on to your childhood,
you may just be right.
Merry Christmas to all,
and, to all, a good night.

...with profound apologies to Clement C. Moore.

*****

WHAT'S IN A NAME?

Boerne ... Helotes ... Niederwald ... Buda ... Polly's Peak ... Fredericksburg - all well-known place names from the Texas Hill Country. But have you ever wondered how these places got their names? Some of the stories behind the names are as unique as the locations themselves.

Boerne, like many German-settled communities, is named for an early pioneer. Ludwig Boerne was a German writer and poet who had become a political refugee before moving to Texas and founding the community that now bears his name. Actually, the current city grew out of an earlier settlement called Tusculum, which was laid out in 1841 but abandoned some ten years later.

Fredericksburg was also established by a well-known German pioneer. In 1846, John O. Meusebach led a wagon train of immigrants north from New Braunfels to establish the new community. Early residents decided that the city should be named in honor of Prince Frederick of Prussia - hence Fredericksburg.

The hamlet of Pipe Creek in Bandera County got it's name from a lost pipe. During a trip to Boerne many years ago, three men stopped along the creek to eat lunch. One of the men later discovered that he had apparently lost his favorite pipe during the stop.

During the return trip, the men found the lost pipe laying in the stream near where they had stopped to eat. As a result, they named the stream Pipe Creek. When a post office was later established near this site, it adopted the name of the creek.

The Kendall County settlement of Bergheim, like so many places in the Hill Country, reflects it's German heritage. Pioneer Andreas Engel suggested the name, which means "home of the hills", when he settled the area in 1887.

Although several stories exist about the naming of Comfort, also in Kendall County, the most widely-accepted story explains that when the first settlers arrived at the site between Cypress Creek and the Guadalupe River, they decided that this was a "gemutlicher platzt" to live. The German word "gemutlich" translates as comfortable. That was later shortened to Comfort.

Buda, in Hays County, seems to be linked

to a poor translation of the Spanish name for widow. Again, several variations of the story continue to circulate, but the most prominent explanation is that the name was inspired by a widow ("viuda" in Spanish) who operated a hotel during the early days of the settlement. Early city fathers decided to name the town Buda, an apparent misspelling of "viuda".

Polly's Peak, the site in Bandera County where the legendary Maiden of Bandera is said to have appeared to bring peace between the settlers and Indians, is not named for anyone named Polly. The peak is actually named for Jose Policarpo Rodrigues, an early hunter, scout, and Indian fighter. It is said that the "Polly" was a nickname derived from Rodrigues' middle name.

Contrary to the belief of many, the Bexar County town of Helotes was not founded by either Willie Nelson or John T. Floore. It is said that the first home in the area was built by a man called Chaca, who cultivated the area into a corn field. Helotes eventually derived it's name from the Indian word (later borrowed by the Spanish) for corn - specifically "green roasting ear of corn".

Niederwald, another German settlement, translates into "lower wood" or "under brush". This Hays County town was settled about 1900 and the name refers to low stands of mesquite trees found in abundance by the early colonists.

Animals, too, have inspired some colorful names. Hogholler Creek in Llano County and Hog Wallow Creek in Medina County both were named, quite simply, because wild hogs were plentiful in these areas.

Fly Gap is said to have been named by a group of settlers whose horses were attacked so badly by a swarm of flies that the poor animals were left covered with blood. Today, this Mason County community continues to bear the name that commemorates a fly swarm.

So, what's in a name? These names are a reflection of the history, heritage, and humor of the resilient pioneers who first settled the hardscrabble hillsides of this region. They are as special, and as unique, as the Texas Hill Country itself.

*****

A PLACE IN TIME

One afternoon not long ago, I found myself hopelessly stuck in a traffic jam on the north side of San Antonio during a rainstorm. Seeking shelter from the storm, flooded streets, and San Antonio drivers who think rain is an open invitation to turn public streets into a demolition derby, I found myself being drawn into a safe haven by a neon beacon from another era.

At the intersection of McCullough Avenue and Hildebrand Road, the Olmos Pharmacy stood like a sentinel, beckoning weary commuters to abandon the rush-hour traffic and return to a time of banana splits with everything on top, or sharing a root beer float with two straws. Through the pharmacy's rain-streaked window, the glowing neon read "fountain".

"Could it be?" I asked myself. "Are there really still drug stores with honest-to-goodness fountains left in this world?"

Inside, I found everything one might expect in a drug store - provided the drug store was in the year 1956.

A huge, old Toledo scale stood just inside the front door, inviting you to check your weight for only a nickel. In the back, a pharmacist was busily dispensing pills and kindly advice to customers he obviously knew. He never seemed to hurry, always taking extra time to carefully explain the prescriptions he was filling.

The pharmacy was carefully stocked to provide for the health-care needs of its customers, but without the frills found in huge, modern pharmacies. There were no barbecue pits, auto parts, or lawn furniture. There was, however, the finest fountain and lunch counter I've seen this side of the 1950's.

I seated myself at the counter and was immediately greeted by a waitress in a crisp white uniform with a name tag that read "Edna". In the back, the cook was artfully flipping hamburgers from the grill, depositing them into those familiar red and green plastic baskets that once adorned lunch counters across America.

The waitress and cook seemed to know everyone, greeting customers by name with a smile and a wave. The fountain provided a warm and welcome atmosphere, unlike the hostility of the wet, angry city just outside.

As I scanned the menu, I noticed that the most expensive thing listed was the lunch special. It included a meat, two vegetables, a small salad, a roll, and tea for only $4.50.

In addition to the plate lunches, burgers, and sandwiches, the fountain offered an abundance of ice cream treats that would tempt Richard Simmons to kick his diet. I ordered the first real fountain Coke I'd had in twenty years.

"It must be 1:30," Edna called back to the cook as she spotted an elderly man making his way through the rain. "Here comes Mr. Frank."

The cook quickly began preparing a plate lunch as Edna placed a glass of iced tea on the counter two stools down from me. As the old man reached the door, the cook was putting the day's luncheon special next to the tea.

"Afternoon, Mr. Frank," the waitress smiled as the elderly gent settled onto the stool in front of the meal. "Thought you might be late today, with this rain and all."

Edna took the man's hat and coat as the cook wiped his hands on his apron and began to chat with his newly-arrived customer. When Edna stopped to ask if I would like a refill, I asked about their elderly customer.

"Mr. Frank is one of our regulars," Edna explained. "He comes in here just about every day at 1:30 for lunch. He always takes the lunch special, no matter what we're serving."

She went on to explain that just about everyone at the pharmacy had worked there for years, and they all knew the regular customers.

Mr. Frank was a widower who lived alone in a small apartment nearby.

"Some days, when the weather's too bad or Mr. Frank isn't feeling well, he calls in and we deliver his lunch over to his house," she told me.

"You mean you actually deliver meals?" I asked.

"Sure we do," Edna said. "We've got a delivery boy that takes medicine to the folks who can't come in, so why not deliver a good hot meal?"

I sat nursing my Coke, watching as the customers came and went. Some were obviously regulars; with others, you couldn't tell. Either way, they were all treated like family come to visit.

I took my time finishing the drink, remembering all the summer afternoons of my childhood when I would stop at just such a drug store fountain for an ice cream sundae. As I finally got up to leave, Mr. Frank and the cook were still deep in conversation. Both seemed to enjoy passing the time with one another.

"You sure you want to go back out in that rain?" Edna asked as I paid the bill. "You're welcome to stay until it lets up."

I thanked her for the offer, but explained that I had to be going. But before walking out, I took one last look around just to make sure it was all real.

There aren't too many places like the Olmos Pharmacy left - a place to find what you need to mend the body and heal the soul.

*****

MARTHA'S BIRTHDAY

Some people go to the cemetery because they have to... some go out of a feeling of obligation... some go out of curiosity... some go out of love... I learned this during a chance meeting one cold winter's day in a small cemetery near the Hill Country community of Bulverde.

The bone-chilling wind whipped the old man's heavy coat as he walked into the cemetery. A blue norther with freezing rain had blown in the day before and the ice-coated ground crunched beneath his feet. As the only other person among the collection of frigid tombstones, I could not help but wonder what brought the old man out in the bitter chill.

The elderly gent carried a paper bag as he made his way to a small plot with a solitary headstone. The grave was simple, but obviously well-tended. The old man seated himself upon a stone bench, seemingly drained from the walk and the bitter cold.

"What a poor soul," I thought to myself. "Why would he come to such a bleak place on a day like this?"

I wondered momentarily if he might be lost. Could the confusion of age, or the bitter cold, have caused him to lose his way and this was the first place he could find to rest?

Then the old man stood and removed a bouquet of roses - yellow roses - from the paper bag. Even from a distance, it was obvious that the roses were the cheap plastic kind found in a five-and-dime store, but he handled them with delicate care. Gently, tenderly he arranged them in the vase on the grave; the arrangement providing the only splash of color against the somber gray of the setting.

As he again seated himself, he pulled his collar tight against the wind. While hesitant to intrude on the old man's solitude, my curiosity overwhelmed me.

"Pardon me," I asked as I approached with uncertainty, "but I couldn't help but notice you here all alone. Is everything all right?"

The old man smiled and motioned for me to have a seat next to him.

"I appreciate your concern," he told me, "but, you see, I'm not really alone. This here's where my Martha rests and I've just come for a little visit."

"Oh, I'm not senile or crazy," he said, apparently noting my puzzled expression. "I know Martha's passed on. But I like to think that, somehow, her spirit knows when I'm here. I shared my thoughts and dreams with her for forty-two years, so after she died I had this bench put here so we could still have our little talks. Seemed only natural to me."

"But why today?" I asked. "It's freezing cold. Couldn't you wait until another day?"

"Absolutely not. Today is Martha's birthday," he informed me. "She always loved yellow roses, so every year I brought her some for her birthday. I still do. They're not real; real ones wouldn't last a minute out here. And those silk roses are just too expensive, so I bring what I can - these artificial plastic roses. I'm sure she understands."

"I come out here almost every weekend. Sometimes I bring new flowers; sometimes I clean the plot; most of the time I just sit and visit. I look forward to these visits."

"Do you think I'm a little nutty?" he abruptly asked.

Words seemed inappropriate, so I just shook my head no.

He pointed to an open spot next to his wife's grave.

"That's my spot; it's all arranged. When I go, all they've got to do is add my name to one side of the gravestone and put me right next to Martha."

"Who'll come to clean the plot and bring flowers then?" I asked.

"I really don't know. Maybe no one. But

Martha and I, we'll be together, so it really doesn't matter."

The chilling cold was cutting through my coat, but the old man didn't seem to feel it. I rose to leave and asked if I could offer him a ride. He thanked me but said he wanted to sit and visit a while longer.

I glanced back as I walked off. The old man didn't look so pitiful now. It was still bitterly cold, the wind still whipped through the stillness of the cemetery, but I didn't feel sorry for him anymore.

He and Martha were together.

*****

BIG OMA

After turning the water glasses from lunch upside-down to drain on the white dishtowel, Big Oma would get her blue-cotton bonnet from the nail by the door and leave her cool kitchen for the hot afternoon sun. It was her time to tend the garden.

Big Oma was my great-grandmother. Since my grandmother was "Oma", I needed a name for my great-grandmother. Because I was still struggling to understand the difference between German and English, I ended up calling her Big Oma. This was the name I would call her for the rest of her life.

Big Oma was a plump, smiling woman who dearly loved the simple things in life. She loved her little garden; she loved her family; and she loved animals, except for the rattlesnakes that sought refuge from the hot sun in her garden. Her favorite snack was butter-bread and a slice of watermelon.

No matter how hot the day, or how withering the sun, Big Oma would don her sunbonnet, grab her trusty hoe, and head out to work in the garden after lunch. She would weed, gathering snap beans into her apron pockets as she went, with her German Shepherd, Boots, trailing behind. Boots would faithfully follow, row after row, moving behind Big Oma like a loyal honor guard.

Both enjoyed their time in the garden. Big Oma could busy her hands with the steady job of picking beans, leaving her mind free to play among old, pleasant memories of years gone by. The wrinkles of her mouth would pucker, matching the inner-rhythm of her thoughts.

Boots, ever watchful of his mistress, would enjoy sporting about in the sun and finding his own idle amusements in the clumps of vines and sweet-smelling dirt. His play would always stop when he perceived a threat to Big Oma. The playful dog quickly became a formidable guardian.

Many a rattlesnake went to its reward for foolishly resting beneath a cool cantaloupe vine in Big Oma's garden. Boots would bark furiously, alerting Big Oma to the danger. Big Oma, never to be intimidated by a mere Diamondback Rattler, quickly dispatched the snake with her trusty hoe.

After the day's work in the little garden

was done, Big Oma and Boots would sit on the front porch and look out over their tillage with the serenity that comes from a job well-done. They enjoyed the comforting "clack-clack" of the windmill turning lazily in the evening breeze. They were serenaded by the long, mournful calls of the doves as the setting sun glistened over the garden. They enjoyed the friendly intimacy of dusk falling over the little farm.

When Big Oma had her stroke, the doctors decided she could no longer live alone on the little farm she loved so. The family agreed, and decided that Big Oma would be placed in a nursing home. Boots would be "adopted" out to the family that lived next to Big Oma's farm.

She spent her final years in an antiseptic nursing home next to a noisy highway in New Braunfels. Instead of the company of a loyal old dog, Big Oma was thrown into the company of strangers. The obvious frailties of those around her only painfully reminded her of her own declining condition.

Instead of the sweet smell of her garden, Big Oma smelled "hospital" smells. The quiet, soothing sounds of the doves in the evening were replaced by the rumble of trucks passing on the highway. Sitting on her porch in the evening as the sun set over her garden was exchanged for sitting on a small, concrete patio with a view of the back side of a bowling alley.

Big Oma knew that death was a constant visitor in this place. She also knew that, sometime soon, she would receive a visit. Big Oma died in that nursing home - a place that was a so foreign to the life she lived that it was beyond her comprehension.

I often think that it would have been better if she could have died on her small farm, near her little garden, on some warm day with the birds singing from the pecan trees. Her last hours would have been spent with Boots sitting dutifully by, and being comforted by the sound of the windmill pumping the cool well-water through the rows of her garden.

There, she would not have died among strangers but, rather, in her rightful place. She would have still been aware of all of the small wonders that she had known from her childhood days: the breeze moving through the pecan trees, the bark of a loyal old dog at play, the distant sound of a sheep's bell coming from across the pasture.

Dying out there, on some bright Hill Country day, Big Oma could have had the funeral she would have wanted, attended by all of those she knew and loved so well: the mourning doves to sing a mournful tune, the windmill to turn out somber, benedictive sighs, and Boots to lie quietly by her side and mourn.

But that didn't happen. My family felt it was best for Big Oma to spend her last days in a nursing home. They felt it was "better for everyone" that way. None of them had "the time" to take her in. Instead, they decided it was "best" to take Big Oma away from the Texas Hill Country that she knew and loved.

It's the only time I've truly been ashamed of my family.

*****

ABOUT THE AUTHOR

John L. Pape

John Pape is best known as the author of "Hill Country Chronicles", a popular weekly column appearing in newspapers in the Texas Hill Country. Pape is a native of Central Texas, and "Hill Country Chronicles" draws heavily on his personal experiences of growing up in rural Texas.

Pape has also written numerous feature magazine articles which have appeared in such publications as the Texas Observer, Gulf Coast Golfer, American Rose, the FBI Law Enforcement Bulletin, and many others.

An honors graduate of the University of Alabama, Pape was recognized as one of the Five Outstanding Young Texans of 1987, as well as one of the Outstanding Young Men of America that same year. He has also been honored as Man of the Year by the City of Mercedes, Texas.

When not writing, Pape is President and CEO of Pape & Associates, a company which provides professional and academic consulting services.

NEL-MAR Publishing

We here at Nel-Mar Publishing would like to extend our thanks to John Pape for giving us the opportunity to publish this book. We have enjoyed working on this book as well as working with John.

Our company is located in the heart of the Texas Hill Country on Canyon Lake. Many of these stories are about our immediate area, and they stir up many memories for all of us.

Thanks again, John, for the pleasure, and I hope your other readers will get as big of a kick out of this book as I have.

Jeff Eberspacher
Managing Editor

Editor's note:
This book is printed on recycled paper. Both the author and the publisher are avid outdoorsmen and appreciate any effort to help clean up our environment. We are trying to do our part.